Sumı

Of

The 4 Hour Body
by Tim Ferriss

An Uncommon Guide
to Rapid Fat-Loss, Incredible Sex,
and Becoming Superhuman

PrimeInsight Press

Note to Readers:

This summary book is not intended to serve as a replacement for the original text but rather is designed to complement the original work, "4-Hour Body" by Tim Ferriss. This is an unofficial summary meant exclusively for educational and personal purposes. It has not been authorized, endorsed, licensed, or approved by the original book's author, publisher, or any of their licensees or affiliates. However, we sincerely believe that our intention is transparent: readers can use this book as a companion to the original, not as a substitute. Please be aware that companion books are within the boundaries of the law.

Published by PrimeInsight Press
First Edition (2023)

TABLE OF CONTENTS

Introduction

In today's fast-paced world, where time is at a premium, the quest for optimum health and well-being might seem like an elusive goal. But what if I told you that a groundbreaking solution exists, one that empowers you to supercharge your vitality in just four hours a week? Welcome to the world of "The 4-Hour Body" by Tim Ferriss, a transformative guide that invites you to embark on an extraordinary journey of self-improvement.

This book is your passport to a realm of possibilities that defy conventional wisdom. It spans a diverse range of topics, from shedding excess weight to sculpting lean muscle, from enhancing your sexual performance to unlocking the secrets of longevity. With a keen eye for the scientific and a pragmatic approach, Ferriss provides an abundance of innovative techniques and strategies to help you achieve remarkable results.

Through "The 4-Hour Body," you'll challenge your preconceived notions about health and well-being, unveiling new pathways to unleash your full potential. It's an open invitation to embrace a paradigm shift in your understanding of what's achievable in the realm of personal health and fitness. Get ready to unearth the hidden keys to leading a healthier, happier, and more fulfilling life, and all within the confines of just four hours a week.

Within the pages of this book, your body becomes a potent ally on your quest to reach the extraordinary. It's an exploration of boundless possibilities and a testament to the notion that, with the right knowledge and approach, you can craft a life that defies mediocrity and embraces excellence. Welcome to "The 4-Hour Body" – a roadmap to unlocking your potential and embracing a life well-lived.

Overview of "The 4-Hour Body" by Timothy Ferriss

Reading Time: 3 mins 37 secs

"The 4-Hour Body" by Tim Ferriss is a comprehensive lifestyle guide that covers various aspects of living life to the fullest. It provides insights into nutrition for weight management, effective exercise routines, optimizing morning rituals, enhancing sexual performance, accelerating injury recovery, and much more. The book serves as an illuminating resource for those seeking to improve various facets of their lives.

The Concept of Minimum Effective Dose
Ferriss introduces the concept of the Minimum Effective Dose (MED), emphasizing that the smallest action required to achieve a specific outcome is the most efficient. Whether it's fat loss or muscle gain, the principle is clear: do just enough to trigger the necessary hormonal responses, as excess effort doesn't necessarily yield better results.

Rules That Challenge the Norm
Ferriss challenges conventional wisdom and urges readers to see everything, including food, as a potential "drug." He differentiates between physical recreation and targeted exercise, underlining the importance of precision in training to attain specific results. His book advises on strategic overeating to expedite progress and defies the notion that genetics dictate destiny. Ferriss also critiques fitness industry jargon used to hype workouts, reminding us that not all calories are equal and that common goals unite men and women when it comes to fitness and dieting.

Starting from Ground Zero

Ferriss acknowledges that following advice can be challenging without a compelling reason for action. Tracking one's progress, even minimally, increases awareness and drives behavioral change. Monitoring one's body composition, rather than just weight, is recommended as it provides a more accurate measure of progress.

Transforming from Images to Action
Ferriss introduces principles for making lifestyle changes foolproof. He encourages conscious choices, gamifies progress tracking, fosters competitiveness, and advocates for small and temporary modifications to habits.

Shedding Excess Fat
The book outlines rules for effective fat loss, emphasizing the avoidance of specific carbohydrates, repetitive meal choices, calorie-free beverages, and even fruit. A weekly "cheat day" is proposed to accommodate dietary indulgence. Ferriss provides an example meal plan and highlights common errors to avoid.

Damage Control: Preventing Fat Gain
Ferriss offers four principles to prevent fat gain during overeating, including insulin control, stomach-emptying acceleration, and muscle contraction. He introduces the "Four Horsemen of Fat Loss," a supplement regimen designed to support weight management.

Mastering Temperature for Weight Control
Manipulating body temperature, specifically through cold exposure, is presented as a method for weight reduction. Cold showers, for example, can boost metabolism and offer additional health benefits.

Balancing Glucose Levels
Ferriss emphasizes the role of maintaining blood glucose levels below 100mg/dL for effective fat loss. Practical strategies include

consuming unsaturated fats, eating slowly, and experimenting with cinnamon and lemon juice. The book acknowledges that some may turn to steroids for extreme fat reduction.

Building Muscle
More muscle makes it easier to maintain lower body fat levels. Ferriss introduces kettlebells as an efficient tool for full-body workouts. He also outlines a six-minute daily ab routine for muscle development and provides an exercise program for mass gain.

Enhancing Sexual Pleasure
Ferriss underscores the importance of understanding and exploring sexual satisfaction. While men can facilitate women's pleasure, women should explore their own orgasmic potential. The book offers advice on sexual pleasure enhancement.

Optimizing Sleep
Quality sleep is essential for a healthy life. Ferriss recommends consuming protein and fiber before bedtime for better sleep quality. He also explores methods such as cold showers and sleeping in short cycles to improve sleep patterns.

Running Faster and Farther
Ferriss delves into research on improving running performance, emphasizing the benefits of warm-up exercises and high-intensity interval training. He simplifies strength training to four key exercises: squats, bench presses, deadlifts, and weightlifting competitions.

Extending Lifespan
The book highlights the potential benefits of calorie reduction for longevity. It also delves into the idea that limiting sperm release could contribute to increased lifespan, drawing from studies in nematodes. Donating blood is suggested as a means to remove excess iron and potentially extend life.

START HERE_THINNER, BIGGER, FASTER

Reading Time: 3 mins 14 secs

The first chapter, "Thinner, Bigger, Faster, Stronger," primarily equips you with the tools to reshape your body for improved performance in a short span.

One of the key focal points is weight loss, aiming to shed body fat. The book illustrates how to apply the 80/20 principle to maximize results and suggests suitable diet programs for weight loss.

Another key area is gaining muscle mass. The text offers advice on bulking up with minimal effort, for instance, with specific nutritional labels for a low-carb diet or with brief, high-intensity weightlifting workouts

Boosting strength is another vital topic tackled in the text. The book presents an effective training program to enhance physical strength, suitable for beginners and experienced individuals alike.

Moreover, the text outlines the practice of the 80/20 principle in various other aspects of daily life, such as stress management, offering techniques to minimize time spent on seemingly useful but ultimately unproductive activities.

Nutrition and dietary habits are another significant theme. It provides guidance on how to enhance eating habits to maximize health benefits and maintain a well-balanced daily diet.

The chapter dedicated to sleep is particularly valuable for those struggling with sleep problems. The text explains how to reduce the adverse impact of sleep disorders on daily well-being, with effective tips to enhance sleep quality through considerations like temperature, reduced light exposure, and noise.

Finally, there are sections addressing blood analysis and medical tests that can help monitor progress and detect potential health issues. The book offers useful information on which blood tests should be conducted to assess health and how to interpret the results.

In summary, the text offers in-depth and detailed resources for body reshaping, strength enhancement, and improved physical performance, all based on the 80/20 principle, which means achieving maximum results with minimal effort and time. Additionally, it aids in stress management, dietary habits, sleep, and health through blood tests.

The text includes a section on speeding up metabolism, considered crucial for weight loss by many. It explains how metabolism works and provides tips on how to accelerate it, such as by consuming smaller, frequent meals and including specific foods in your diet.

Various exercise techniques are explored, including high-intensity training and weightlifting. Weightlifting, in particular, is seen as an effective way to build muscle mass and enhance overall body strength. The text also provides advice on improving exercise technique to prevent injuries.

Intermittent fasting is also covered in a section of the book. This dietary practice, involving alternating periods of eating with fasting, is explained in detail, offering information on how it works and its potential health benefits.

The text also presents various specific diets and dietary regimes, such as the "Slow-Carb" diet, a balanced diet suitable for weight loss. The book provides a complete meal plan to successfully follow it, along with meal preparation strategies.

There are also sections dedicated to injury prevention and recovery. The text suggests specific warm-up exercises and offers tips to prevent injuries, as well as methods and techniques for speeding up recovery and getting back to physical activity more quickly.

Finally, the book offers suggestions for improving body posture, reducing pain, and preventing muscle and joint issues. It provides specific exercises to enhance body alignment and correct any postural problems.

In summary, the text covers a wide range of secondary topics, all based on scientific evidence and aimed at improving health and well-being. These topics include metabolism acceleration, various exercise techniques, intermittent fasting, specific diets, injury prevention and recovery, as well as tips for posture improvement.

FUNDAMENTALS—FIRST AND FOREMOST

Reading Time: 4 mins 10 secs

THE MINIMUM EFFECTIVE DOSE

The fundamental concept that Ferriss introduces in this subchapter is "The Minimum Effective Dose" (MED) and the importance of identifying the minimum quantity of an agent needed to achieve the desired result. The author emphasizes that anything beyond the MED is a waste of time and effort, and that the central goal is to achieve results with the least effort possible.

Ferriss illustrates the MED concept with various examples, including the process of boiling water: once the MED is reached, raising the temperature no longer increases the rate of water evaporation but merely results in an energy surplus. Similarly, he highlights how sun exposure, once the MED is attained, leads to tanning, but exceeding this quantity only results in skin burning.

The first secondary topic that Ferriss addresses concerns the overload of available information. He argues that the abundance of information often distracts us from achieving our goals, leading us into a "choice paradox" where we feel overwhelmed by the decision to make. Ferriss states that to avoid this, we should choose the simplest path to reach our goals by identifying the MED. This way, distractions are minimized, and focus is directed towards the desired outcomes.

Another secondary point by Ferriss is the necessity of focusing on the end goal rather than the activity itself. Often, people concentrate solely on the activity without a clear idea of the ultimate result they want to achieve. Ferriss suggests defining the end goal clearly and concentrating on the activities required to reach it. This approach prevents wasting time and energy on activities that won't lead to the desired outcome and ensures that every action is aimed at achieving the goal.

A third secondary topic relates to the concept of "on-ramps." Ferriss explains that on-ramps are the initial activities that allow us to enter a new routine. To successfully establish a new habit, a good on-ramp is necessary, one that is easy to perform and requires little time and effort. This way, it's possible to create a routine that becomes automatic within a few weeks, enabling the adoption of positive and lasting habits.

In summary, the subchapter on "The Minimum Effective Dose" focuses on the importance of identifying the minimum amount of effort needed to achieve your goals. Ferriss illustrates this concept through various examples and stresses the importance of focusing on the end goal, avoiding distractions, and planning the necessary activities to reach it. Finally, the author describes the concept of "on-ramps" and how they can help create new habits more effectively and durably.

RULES THAT CHANGE THE RULES

The text primarily focuses on the effective methods for weight loss and muscle growth. The author provides numerous examples of popular theories on weight loss and muscle growth that lack scientific evidence, such as extreme diets and intense physical workouts. Instead, the author suggests adopting an approach based on "The Minimum Effective Dose" (MED), which encourages choosing the most effective activities and expending minimal physical effort to achieve the desired goal.

Another important secondary topic in the text is strategies for changing one's mental model. The author argues that limiting beliefs about weight loss can hinder one from achieving their goals, and some of these beliefs can be transformed into beliefs that serve their objectives.

The text "RULES THAT CHANGE THE RULES" underscores the importance of critical data analysis and a deep understanding of how one's body functions. For instance, the author discusses the importance of knowing one's body fat percentage and monitoring their diet and level of physical activity to reach the desired results.

Another topic addressed in the text relates to the importance of choosing the right words to describe weight loss goals. The author recommends avoiding terms like "toning" and "shaping," which lack a scientific basis, and suggests using precise language based on measurable parameters.

Lastly, the text provides an overview of testimonials from those who have used the MED approach to achieve their weight loss and muscle gain goals. Success stories include people who have lost weight quickly and those who have achieved greater results with minimal effort. This demonstrates how the MED approach can be an extremely effective method for losing weight and gaining muscle without having to follow strict diets or engage in intense physical exercise.

In summary, the text "RULES THAT CHANGE THE RULES" offers a comprehensive overview of effective methods for weight loss and muscle gain, suggesting an approach based on the MED concept and emphasizing the importance of precise language and critical data analysis to achieve the desired results.

GROUND ZERO

Reading Time: 5 mins 11 secs

THE HARAJUKU MOMENT

The "THE HARAJUKU MOMENT" subchapter starts off by stressing the importance of having an eye-opening moment, an "Harajuku Moment," that pushes a person to transform a desirable goal into a personal obligation. The author highlights that many people fail to achieve lasting results because they lack sufficient motivation. This chapter focuses on the significance of having a profound reason to pursue a goal.

The author explores two primary approaches to goal pursuit. The first involves maintaining a constant reminder of the desired goal. Using numerical data is suggested as an effective way to stay consistently motivated, as it provides a tangible reference for the progress made towards the goal. Additionally, the author advises seeking inspiration from people who have already achieved similar goals by learning from their experiences.

A tangible example of a "Harajuku Moment" is presented through the case of Chad Fowler. Chad had struggled to improve his physical fitness for years without success, but after making a radical decision and having an enlightening moment, he managed to lose around 70 pounds in less than 12 months. Fowler's case is used to highlight how the use of numerical data can be an effective source of motivation. Furthermore, the author provides a link to a video that illustrates his personal Harajuku Moment.

The subchapter concludes with the author's urging to find strong and genuine motivation for pursuing one's goals, by exposing oneself to the experiences of people who have already achieved similar results. The author also suggests creating a system that supports the maintenance of constant motivation, through the use of numerical data, such as weight loss or physical performance improvement, for instance.

In summary, the "THE HARAJUKU MOMENT" subchapter presents a series of related topics regarding the importance of having strong and constant motivation in pursuing one's goals. The author suggests using constant reminders, like numerical data, to establish a connection with one's objectives, creating a personal support network, and seeking inspiration from experienced individuals. Chad Fowler is presented as an example of how a Harajuku Moment and numerical data can be used to positively change one's life.

ELUSIVE BODYFAT

In the "ELUSIVE BODYFAT" subsection of "55-102 GROUND ZERO," the author delves into various key aspects related to body fat and weight loss, offering some pretty helpful insights and tips.

First off, it's emphasized that body fat isn't distributed evenly. You've got that visceral fat hanging out around your internal organs, and that's a big no-no because it can increase your risk of some serious health issues like heart disease, diabetes, and high blood pressure. The text suggests specific exercises to tackle visceral fat and outlines dietary recommendations to help you shed those extra pounds.

Another important point is the approach to weight loss. The author stresses the need to avoid an overly aggressive or unrealistic approach to weight loss, which can be harmful to your body. Instead, it's advised to aim for long-term physical well-being with a balanced workout regimen that also focuses on building muscle, not just shedding body fat.

Lastly, the "ELUSIVE BODYFAT" subsection touches on the significance of inspiration and motivation in your weight loss journey. Finding motivation from friends, family, or a coach, as well as seeking support from a community or group, can be incredibly helpful. Plus, identifying those pivotal turning points in your fitness journey – those 'Harajuku moments' – can serve as great sources of renewed motivation.

So, in a nutshell, "ELUSIVE BODYFAT" in "55-102 GROUND ZERO" gives you a wealth of insightful information on losing weight and dealing with body fat. It covers various critical secondary issues too, like how fat gets distributed in your body, your approach to workouts and weight loss, and the significance of motivation and inspiration.

FROM PHOTOS TO FEAR

In the section "FROM PHOTOS TO FEAR" of the chapter "GROUND ZERO," we dive into the nifty practice of using photos as a way to track your weight loss journey and see the tangible results of your exercise efforts. The author emphasizes just how crucial it is to have a quantitative and concrete approach to monitoring your fitness progress, and using photos can be a powerful tool to achieve this.

More specifically, the author recommends taking pictures of your body from various angles and positions. By using different angles and perspectives, you can precisely analyze how your training is affecting specific parts of your body, capturing even the smallest changes that might be hard to notice otherwise.

The text underscores that photos can provide a more effective way of gauging the impact of your training compared to other methods like just hopping on the scale or measuring your body circumferences. With photos, you can immediately visualize the effects of your workouts on specific areas and get an overall picture of your fitness progress.

It's also crucial to take these photos consistently and regularly, ideally in the same spot and at the same time. This way, you can easily compare and analyze your progress, ensuring that your results are easily comparable over time.

To take these photos, the author suggests using your smartphone or a regular camera in a suitable environment with good lighting. You can even snap them weekly to track your progress during specific weeks. Furthermore, it's a good idea to compile these photos in a journal or a designated app to give you a comprehensive overview of your fitness journey and your progress over time.

In summary, using photographs is an extremely effective method to monitor your weight loss process and concretely assess the results of your training. By analyzing these photos, you can observe improvements in your body and assess your fitness activity precisely and tangibly.

SUBTRACTING FAT basics

Reading Time: 13 mins 6 secs

THE SLOW-CARB DIET I

In "THE SLOW-CARB DIET I" the focus is on detailing the Slow-Carb Diet and how to effectively lose weight. It begins by highlighting the potential to lose up to 20 pounds in a month without exercise, citing an example of someone who shed around 15 pounds in six weeks following the diet.

The section goes on to lay out the fundamental principles of the Slow-Carb Diet, emphasizing what to eat and what to avoid while on the regimen. The diet is based on five core rules: eliminating white carbohydrates, consuming protein at every meal, refraining from drinking calories, eating legumes and vegetables with each meal, and indulging in a cheat day once a week.

An extensive examination of carbohydrates is carried out, categorizing them into slow carbohydrates (found in legumes and vegetables) and fast carbohydrates (found in refined flours and sugars). This classification guides food choices during the diet.

The text delves further into the topic of fats, distinguishing between harmful fats (like trans-fats) and healthy fats (such as omega-3 and omega-6 fatty acids). This approach allows the Slow-Carb Diet to balance the goals of weight loss with maintaining a wholesome and nourishing diet.

A list of recommended foods during the Slow-Carb Diet is provided, including protein sources like eggs, meat, fish, and legumes, as well as vegetables like broccoli, spinach, asparagus, and tomatoes, and berries such as blueberries and raspberries.

The text concludes with a collection of success stories from individuals who have followed the Slow-Carb Diet, achieving remarkable results in terms of weight loss and overall health and well-being.

In addition to the primary topics addressed in the "THE SLOW-CARB DIET I", several secondary but important subtopics are discussed:

1. Proteins: Further details on recommended lean protein sources such as chicken, fish, or lean meats are provided, with guidance to avoid fatty proteins like bacon or sausages.

2. Prohibited Foods: A list of foods that must be avoided during the diet, including bread, pasta, rice, potatoes, refined sugars, carbonated beverages, and fruit juices, is presented.

3. Legume Preparation: The text explains how to prepare legumes to make them more digestible and appetizing, recommending soaking them for at least 24 hours and using spices to enhance the flavor.

4. Cheat Day: Unlike other diets, the Slow-Carb Diet allows for a cheat day once a week, where one can consume whatever they desire without restrictions. This day serves to maintain a high metabolism and prevent weight loss plateaus.

5. Bodybuilding Champion Testimonial: A bodybuilding champion's testimony about how he utilized the Slow-Carb Diet to minimize body fat percentage is featured.

6. Weekend and Travel Adjustments: The sottocapitolo offers additional advice on how to adapt the Slow-Carb Diet during weekends and while traveling, suggesting various strategies to avoid consuming unhealthy foods during particularly challenging periods.

These secondary subtopics offer a more comprehensive understanding of how the Slow-Carb Diet operates and how one can effectively pursue their weight loss and overall health goals.

THE SLOW-CARB DIET II

In "THE SLOW-CARB DIET II," the text delves deeper into the Slow-Carb Diet, offering numerous insights to help you navigate this dietary regimen for optimal results.

To begin, it answers some of the most frequently asked questions about the Slow-Carb Diet. For instance, it clarifies that this diet isn't just about reducing overall carbohydrate intake but primarily focuses on avoiding high glycemic index carbohydrates. These are the types that cause a rapid spike in blood sugar levels, potentially leading to fat accumulation.

The text then suggests a gradual approach to adopting the Slow-Carb Diet. It recommends starting by substituting only your breakfast with a Slow-Carb breakfast and then transitioning to a full Slow-Carb diet for six days a week. This 'training' phase helps your body acclimate to the Slow-Carb Diet, reducing the risk of abandoning it after just a few days.

Additionally, the text provides numerous tips to overcome the challenges that may arise during the diet. For instance, to combat carbohydrate and sweet cravings, it advises the consumption of protein-rich foods or liquids like green tea and coffee.

The concept of a "cheat day" is further explored, wherein you're allowed to consume foods outside the Slow-Carb Diet for one day a week. The text recommends various techniques to minimize the impact of a cheat day, such as choosing high-protein foods to limit sugar and carbohydrate absorption.

In the final section of the chapter, the text delves into managing potential weight gain following a cheat day. It advises following simple rules to sensitize muscle tissue to nutrient intake. This includes avoiding excessive fat consumption, increasing metabolic activity, and reducing insulin release.

In summary, the section "THE SLOW-CARB DIET II" offers a plethora of directives and insights to help you navigate the Slow-Carb Diet effectively. It provides detailed guidance on the principles, techniques, and strategies to achieve the best possible results.

In the "THE SLOW-CARB DIET II" are also explored:

1. High vs. Low Glycemic Carbohydrates: The sottocapitolo explains the critical difference between high and low glycemic index carbohydrates. High glycemic carbs can cause rapid blood sugar spikes and fat accumulation, while low glycemic options, such as those found in vegetables, fruits, and legumes, are digested more slowly, preventing fat storage.

2. Slow-Carb Vegetables and Proteins: Specific Slow-Carb foods are discussed, including leafy green vegetables like spinach, broccoli, and kale, which are low in carbohydrates and rich in vitamins and minerals. The text also suggests various Slow-Carb protein sources like beans, eggs, lean meats, and fish.

3. Foods to Avoid: The author provides a list of foods to steer clear of in the Slow-Carb Diet, such as pasta, bread, and french fries. It explains how these items can lead to blood sugar spikes and fat accumulation.

4. Fluid Intake: The text emphasizes the importance of proper hydration during the Slow-Carb Diet, recommending ample water consumption while limiting sweet beverages like fruit juices and soda. Additionally, it suggests green tea, which contains catechins known to aid in fat burning.

5. Meal Planning and Preparation: The chapter offers insights into meal planning and preparation for the Slow-Carb Diet. It advises planning meals in advance and cooking in large batches to ensure a ready supply of Slow-Carb-compliant foods.

In conclusion "THE SLOW-CARB DIET II" provides a comprehensive array of information related to the Slow-Carb Diet, enabling a healthy and effective adherence to this dietary regimen and offering a well-rounded guide to dietary habits suitable for a balanced lifestyle.

DAMAGE CONTROL

The author addresses three main topics concerning fat gain prevention, what to do when indulging, and tips for maintaining a balanced and healthy diet.

When it comes to fat gain prevention, the author emphasizes the importance of planning for restaurant or party meals. This planning allows you to have a clear understanding of the situation and the room for maneuver you have. The author suggests eating a low-fat snack before going out, reducing your appetite during the event and preventing overindulgence. Water and calorie-free beverages are favored over alcoholic drinks, as the latter diminish an individual's self-regulation capacity. Lastly, the author stresses the importance of concentrating carbohydrate consumption in the first half of the upcoming meal to reduce appetite.

Regarding indulgence strategies, the text advises planning indulgent meals to sample various foods while limiting the quantity of each item. This approach allows you to maintain control during the indulgence and alleviate potential post-indulgence guilt. The author also suggests keeping the upcoming meal as balanced as possible, avoiding skipping previous or subsequent meals and excessive fasting. Lastly, they emphasize the importance of limiting alcohol intake and maintaining portion control with fried foods.

Finally, concerning tips for maintaining a balanced and healthy diet, the author recommends selecting natural, organic, and additive-free foods. They advise avoiding processed foods such as packaged goods, fried items, fast food, cookies, and chips, while favoring simple foods like lean meats, fish, fresh fruits, and vegetables. The author underscores that the Slow-Carb Diet should be considered a guide, not an absolute doctrine, and encourages individuals to modify the rules based on their lifestyle and potential food intolerances.

These pieces of advice can be found starting from page 35. The importance of fat gain prevention, planned indulgence, and maintaining a balanced and healthy diet are fundamental factors for overall health.

Within the section "DAMAGE CONTROL" of the chapter "SUBTRACTING FAT," the author addresses various minor topics and provides additional details on weight control and the maintenance of a healthy lifestyle:

- Planning Meals Away from Home: The author advises against arriving at a restaurant or social event on an empty stomach, as this may lead to overeating and potential weight gain. To prevent this, they suggest having a small pre-event dinner that consists of low-fat, protein-rich foods to keep you satisfied for some time. Furthermore, during the event, the author advises avoiding carbohydrate-heavy dishes and instead opting for an abundance of low-carb vegetables.

- Managing Indulgence: The text suggests planning indulgent meals, known as cheat meals, wherein you allow yourself to consume foods not typically included in your diet, such as pizza or dessert. The key is to limit the quantity consumed and return to a balanced, low-fat eating routine the next day. Additionally, the author recommends engaging in physical activity after the indulgence to expedite food metabolism and prevent abdominal fat accumulation.

- Maintaining a Balanced and Healthy Diet: The author emphasizes that the Slow-Carb Diet should be viewed as a guide rather than an inflexible doctrine. They recommend adapting the diet to personal preferences, including foods that are enjoyed and limiting those that are not. It is crucial to read product labels, avoid processed foods, and favor fresh and wholesome options.

- Managing Breakfast: The author suggests dedicating at least half an hour to breakfast, opting for breakfast items that are centered around lean protein, and adding a portion of low-carb vegetables. Additionally, they recommend drinking at least a glass of room-temperature water. The intake of cereals and flour-based foods is to be limited, favoring legumes such as black beans, kidney beans, and lentils.

Finally, the author underscores the importance of not focusing solely on the Slow-Carb Diet but also incorporating regular physical exercise and ensuring adequate rest for optimal well-being.

In conclusion "DAMAGE CONTROL" offers practical advice for maintaining a proper dietary and exercise regimen, ultimately preventing weight gain. Following these recommendations, along with the Slow-Carb Diet, can ensure steady weight loss, along with the maintenance of optimal health and a healthy lifestyle.

THE FOUR HORSEMEN OF FAT-LOSS

The chapter kicks off with a discussion of what the author dubs "the four horsemen" – four key strategies for shedding fat.

First up is low-carb dieting, where you cut down on carbs and focus more on protein and healthy fats. Contrary to common belief, this approach can be effective for weight loss.

The second horseman is saturated fats, which challenges the usual notion that reducing saturated fat intake equals weight loss. The author advocates for its role in a balanced diet.

The third horseman rides on the importance of proteins, highlighting their significance in maintaining muscle mass and as a long-term energy source.

Last but not least, we have the thermogenic effect of foods – how our bodies use energy to digest and absorb nutrients. This plays a crucial role in weight management.

While these four horsemen are important in the fat-loss journey, they're not the entire solution. So, the chapter goes on to discuss the combined use of PAGG dietary supplements as an extra fat-burning boost. However, there's a missing ingredient in the formula, and it's garlic.

The following section delves into **garlic's impact on fat loss**. It includes an anecdote about a homeless person who claims to have shed over 100 pounds by consuming garlic. Intrigued, the author decides to test the effects of garlic on weight loss, and the results are promising.

It's noted that the benefits of garlic stem from its sulfur compounds, which have antioxidant and anti-inflammatory properties. Garlic can potentially enhance heart health, regulate blood pressure, and cholesterol levels.

Moving on, the chapter describes how **garlic can be incorporated into the PAGG dietary supplement combo**. There's positive feedback from a semi-pro athlete who's experienced the benefits of using a PAGG supplement that includes garlic.

Now, let's explore some secondary points.

Super Cissus Rx, an herbal supplement based on Cissus quadrangularis, is mentioned as a potential appetite suppressant that could deter the formation of new fat cells. This supplement could also enhance athletic performance.

Athletic Greens is introduced as an all-in-one fruit and vegetable alternative with 76 ingredients, including inulin to improve gut health. It's presented as a way to ensure you're getting the right nutrients during the weight loss process.

The chapter goes on to describe the Escali Cesto Portable Nutritional Scale, a portable scale that tracks your daily food intake. It's equipped with a display that provides nutritional information for nearly 1,000 types of food.

Nutrition Data, a website that helps users analyze food recipes and compare nutritional values, is also highlighted. It allows you to calculate calories and nutrients in different portions of a specific food and compare them to your daily calorie needs.

Additionally, the text mentions two types of elastic bands: Thera-Bands and Mini-Bands. These are used for fitness exercises. Thera-Bands come in various colors and are primarily for rehabilitation exercises, while Mini-Bands are resistance bands that weightlifters use to add resistance to squats, bench presses, and deadlifts.

Finally, there's a mention of epigallocatechin gallate (EGCG) found in green tea, which may aid in weight loss due to its antioxidant and metabolism-boosting properties. However, the text cautions that EGCG might interact with certain medications, such as the estrogen antagonist tamoxifen. It's advised to consult a doctor before using it during anti-tumor therapy.

In summary, the chapter titled "THE FOUR HORSEMEN OF FAT-LOSS" sheds light on the intricacies of the fat loss process, offering various tips and possibilities to support your journey. Whether it's through dietary supplements like Cissus quadrangularis, handy nutritional scales like the Escali Cesto Portable Nutritional Scale, fitness exercises with Thera-Bands and Mini-Bands, or controlling and comparing calorie intake via Nutrition Data, there are numerous tools to assist you. Garlic, a potential game-changer in this journey, serves as both a standalone ingredient and a part of PAGG dietary supplements. While it shows promise, more research is needed to fully understand its weight loss effects.

SUBTRACTING FAT Advanced

Reading Time: 7 mins 49 secs

ICE AGE

The "Ice Age" subchapter in the book "Subtracting Fat - Advanced" delves into several captivating topics for those looking to shed pounds and burn fat more efficiently.

First off, it discusses the role of cold in activating brown adipose tissue (BAT) and speeding up metabolism. The text introduces various tools and techniques to activate BAT and ramp up fat burning. This includes ice packs, cold baths, and chilly showers. What's intriguing is that these methods have been used even at a professional level and backed by scientific studies.

Secondly, the subchapter focuses on testosterone and growth hormone – two crucial hormones for muscle development and fat loss. It unveils several techniques to boost the production of these hormones, such as adopting a low-carb diet, weightlifting, and ensuring quality rest.

Next up, it delves into adiponectin, a hormone produced by adipose tissue. Adiponectin plays a vital role in fat burning and enhancing glucose absorption by muscle tissues. The subchapter offers an in-depth understanding of how adiponectin functions and why maintaining steady levels is crucial.

Finally, the "Ice Age" subchapter provides techniques for monitoring blood glucose levels, such as using a glucometer. This tool can be beneficial for those aiming to prevent blood sugar spikes and reduce insulin resistance.

Moreover, the subchapter initially delves into low-carb diets and their role in weight loss and fat breakdown. It suggests adopting a diet rich in proteins and healthy fats like meat, fish, eggs, and nuts while avoiding refined carbs like bread, pasta, and sweets. The importance of reducing sugar and refined grain intake is emphasized since these foods can elevate blood sugar levels and hinder fat loss.

Additionally, the subchapter introduces innovative techniques to increase water intake and maintain proper hydration throughout the day. It suggests using water bottles with hourly markers to ensure adequate water consumption. It also highlights some tips for boosting fluid intake, like drinking unsweetened tea and beverages while avoiding sugary drinks.

The subchapter then emphasizes the significance of physical activity in the weight loss journey. It presents various training techniques, including weightlifting and cardiovascular exercises, stressing the importance of combining these activities to burn fat and boost metabolism. In particular, high-intensity exercises, such as the Tabata method, are introduced, as they can help burn more calories in less time.

Lastly, it discusses "emotional release" as a key factor in maintaining motivation during the weight loss process. It introduces techniques for managing negative emotions and keeping motivation high, such as goal journaling and seeking support from friends and family. It underscores the importance of staying focused on weight loss goals and avoiding distractions or temptations that can interfere with the process.

In conclusion, the "Ice Age" subchapter offers a wealth of information and practical advice for weight loss and fat burning. The author provides in-depth insights and innovative techniques to help readers effectively and sustainably achieve their weight loss goals.

THE GLUCOSE SWITCH

The subchapter titled "THE GLUCOSE SWITCH" in the document emphasizes the importance of controlling blood glucose levels for achieving rapid weight loss. The author provides insights on using the medical device DexCom, which allows real-time monitoring of blood sugar levels to predict how different foods will impact blood glucose. This enables individuals to schedule exercises to maximize weight loss and muscle gain while keeping blood sugar levels below a well-defined threshold.

Crucially, maintaining stable weight loss is also highlighted, as elevated sugar levels can impede the weight loss process. The DexCom device is a valuable tool for measuring the impact of various food sources on blood glucose, aiding in choosing a diet that suits individual needs.

The subchapter also delves into the significance of physical exercise in blood sugar control. The author recommends scheduling high-intensity workouts when blood sugar levels are higher and advises against exercising on an empty stomach. It's stressed how glucose monitoring is vital for those with diabetes, as it assists in regulating insulin intake and sugar levels.

In summary, "THE GLUCOSE SWITCH" subchapter provides practical advice on monitoring blood glucose levels for healthy weight loss. The information is valuable not only for those seeking to lose weight but also for individuals with diabetes who need to regulate blood sugar levels.

The document contains several secondary pieces of useful information on various topics. Notably, a section on page 30 offers valuable tips on airport security, advising against carrying items that may pose issues during security checks. It suggests avoiding sharp objects like knives and opting for items such as a nail file that are generally tolerated by security checks.

The document includes an author's food diary, detailing and illustrating the foods consumed throughout the day and their effects. This section provides insights into the author's diet, which is primarily based on protein-rich foods and healthy fats like meat, eggs, and avocados. The author follows this diet to improve their health and physical performance.

Lastly, the chapter offers a list of online and offline resources for information on supplements, anabolic agents, and reliable sources for obtaining more information on physical performance. It also provides information on injury prevention and post-exercise recovery techniques.

In general, the document has been composed with a practical approach covering a wide range of topics related to health, wellness, and physical performance. The information provided in various subchapters is detailed, offering useful advice for anyone looking to improve their health or physical performance. These insights, such as blood glucose monitoring, dietary recommendations, and exercise techniques, are presented in an organized and reader-friendly manner.

THE LAST MILE

In the section titled "THE LAST MILE," we delve into the art of shedding those last few pounds of body fat using natural methods, steering clear of any chemical interventions. Tim Ferriss kicks things off with an interview featuring bodybuilding guru John Romano, who spills the beans on the major pitfalls encountered by many bodybuilders. One striking revelation is the misconception of being "natural" just because you're downing massive quantities of food. Romano emphasizes the reality that most bodybuilders resort to pharmaceuticals to reach their competitive peak.

Ferriss serves up a plateful of advice on paying attention to the speed of your food's digestion. He suggests savoring each bite by chewing it at least 20 times to slow down digestion and keep those hunger pangs at bay. Moreover, Ferriss highlights the benefits of maintaining blood sugar levels below 100 mg/dL to aid in weight loss. Achieving this involves gradually phasing out certain food categories, such as bread, pasta, and cereals, or reducing their consumption. He also advises against frequent snacking, as it can lead to increased insulin levels, hindering weight loss.

Another critical point of discussion in this subchapter revolves around the significance of IPTA (Interval Power Training Aerobic). Ferriss suggests IPTA workouts to pump up those muscles and give your metabolism a significant boost. The mention of GOPs makes an appearance in this section as a dietary strategy. GOPs involve eliminating high-saturated fat foods like ham and bacon for a healthier, more balanced diet.

Ferriss further explores the value of natural elements such as adiponectin and BAT. Adiponectin, a hormone produced by fat cells, can enhance fat oxidation and glucose uptake in muscle tissues. BAT, on the other hand, is brown adipose tissue that, when activated, kicks into high gear to burn through glucose and lipids to generate heat.

Expanding upon secondary topics, this subchapter touches on the importance of maintaining a high level of hygiene, both in your surroundings and personal habits, to create a healthy environment for your body and mind. Ferriss underscores the use of chemical-free cleaning products for your well-being.

The concept of "carb cycling" also makes its debut, aimed at reactivating your metabolism during a low-calorie diet. Ferriss explains how alternating between low and high-carb days can rev up your metabolism, making your weight loss efforts more effective.

Additionally, the subchapter compiles a list of high-protein, low-saturated fat, and low-carb foods ideal for weight loss and muscle gain. Ferriss endorses items like yogurt, nuts, lean meat, eggs, and fish for their optimal nutrient combinations in a balanced diet.

Exploring the Interval Power Training Aerobic (IPTA) exercise regimen is another key theme. Ferriss underscores the importance of correct IPTA training and provides practical tips for executing this form of exercise effectively and safely.

In essence, "THE LAST MILE" subchapter delivers a wealth of insights into natural techniques for shedding those last stubborn pounds of body fat. Ferriss strongly advocates steering clear of chemical substances and medications, which can pose health risks. Instead, he champions natural methods and dietary strategies to achieve optimal health and fitness.

ADDING MUSCLE

Reading Time: 14 mins 32 secs

BUILDING THE PERFECT POSTERIOR

In the section titled "BUILDING THE PERFECT POSTERIOR," the author imparts valuable insights on how to develop the posterior muscle chain in both men and women. Specifically, for women, it delves into crafting the perfect posterior while shedding substantial amounts of body fat. A central theme of this section revolves around how building this muscle chain can lead to increased strength and sex appeal in less time. The author provides a slew of specific exercises to help achieve this goal.

The section kicks off with a compelling anecdote about a bet among a group of women to see who could lose the highest percentage of body fat in 12 weeks. This motivated Tracy, one of the women involved in the wager, to take control of her lifestyle with a low-carb diet and short kettlebell swing exercises. The author describes kettlebell swings as remarkably effective for building the posterior muscle chain. The text underscores that behavioral change is more critical for altering body composition than adhering to a rigid set of instructions.

Subsequently, the section outlines a four-week test focusing on kettlebell swing exercises and minor dietary adjustments, resulting in significant weight loss and a noticeable reduction in body fat percentage for one woman. Remarkably, the test only entailed three sessions per week, each lasting just five minutes. The author posits that engaging in an entirely different physical activity for a short duration per week can yield significant results.

The author goes on to furnish a series of specific exercises for constructing the posterior muscle chain, elucidating how this can lead to enhanced strength and sex appeal in less time. Notably, the section highlights that the development of the posterior muscle chain is crucial for both men and women, encompassing all muscles from the base of the skull to the Achilles tendons.

Furthermore, it expounds on how building the perfect posterior isn't merely an aesthetic pursuit but offers health benefits such as reduced muscle injuries and increased trunk stability. The author presents a variety of specific exercises for achieving the perfect posterior, including the impactful "kettlebell swings" that significantly contribute to building the posterior muscle chain.

To wrap it up, the "BUILDING THE PERFECT POSTERIOR" section provides a comprehensive deep dive into constructing the posterior muscle chain. It offers a plethora of tips and exercises for both men and women to shape the perfect posterior while gaining greater strength and sex appeal in less time. Additionally, it underscores that small behavioral changes, such as engaging in brief, intense physical activity and adopting a protein-rich morning diet, can translate into substantial body benefits, underscoring the pivotal role of behavioral change in body composition transformation.

One crucial topic is the emphasis on monitoring body fat percentage rather than relying solely on scale weight, as it often provides a more accurate indicator of body composition. The text provides insights on how to accurately measure body fat percentage and suggests employing various measuring tools for precise results.

Another equally vital subject is the kettlebell swing, a central exercise that holds numerous health benefits, including reducing the risk of injuries, enhancing balance and posture, and fortifying the posterior muscle chain. The text offers an in-depth guide on proper kettlebell swing execution, paying close attention to correct technique and breathing.

The section also elucidates how to avoid common exercise mistakes, such as lifting too much weight or executing exercises with improper form. The author provides tips on how to identify and rectify these errors and how to heed the body's warning signals to prevent joint or muscle damage.

The text additionally provides an overview of how small behavioral changes, like engaging in short bursts of physical activity and consuming a protein-rich breakfast, can enhance body composition. The author underscores how these simple changes can yield significant benefits for the body.

In summary, the "BUILDING THE PERFECT POSTERIOR" section offers a comprehensive guide on constructing a powerful posterior muscle chain, crafting the perfect posterior, and achieving greater strength and sex appeal in less time through specific exercises. It also underscores the importance of proper body fat monitoring, correct exercise execution, and behavioral modifications to achieve lasting positive results.

SIX-MINUTE ABS

First and foremost, the text emphasizes the significance of planning and motivation to achieve lasting results. It recommends setting realistic and achievable goals, breaking down the journey into small increments to celebrate frequent successes. Additionally, it suggests tracking progress through continuous monitoring, such as using a scale or keeping a food diary. The text underscores the importance of identifying personal reasons for pursuing fitness goals, which can vary from person to person, whether it's seeking better health, physical attractiveness, or improved mental well-being.

Furthermore, the text offers advice on preventing physical injuries during exercise. It advises selecting exercises appropriate to one's fitness level and avoiding pushing too hard beyond one's limits. It stresses the importance of warming up before exercising and post-workout stretching to prevent muscle micro-injuries. Moreover, the text suggests paying attention to the body's sensations, like muscle soreness or tension, to avoid potential harm.

Lastly, the text highlights the importance of having a moral and social support system to achieve fitness goals. It recommends involving friends or family in physical activities, such as going for a walk together or adopting a new eating style as a group. Engaging in a fitness class provides an opportunity to socialize and meet people who share a passion for fitness.

In summary, the text provides valuable advice for achieving optimal fitness, approaching your goal by scaling your milestones, monitoring your progress, and focusing on your personal motivations for physical and mental well-being. Additionally, it suggests how to avoid muscle injuries and emphasizes the pivotal role of moral and social support as a determining factor for the success of your fitness journey.

FROM GEEK TO FREAK

The section "FROM GEEK TO FREAK" provides a workout program and advice on nutrition and rest for those looking to increase muscle mass and strength.

The author explains how to build an effective training program, emphasizing the use of "forced repetitions" and "negative repetitions" to maximize muscle mass and strength creation. Furthermore, the author underscores the importance of "time under tension" during exercise, which is the time the muscle is under tension during the movement. It's argued that slow, controlled movement is more important than the speed of the repetition itself.

The author then offers a series of specific exercises for muscle mass and strength gain. These include weightlifting and resistance exercises such as "heavy deadlifts" and "weighted chins," among others. These exercises can be performed in alternating sets, ensuring a focus on specific muscle groups and maintaining tension.

The "FROM GEEK TO FREAK" section also provides information on the importance of adequate rest. The author claims that rest is crucial for muscle and strength growth, recommending at least 7 hours of sleep per night.

Regarding nutrition, the author states that a balanced diet is fundamental for increasing muscle mass and strength. The right balance of proteins, carbohydrates, and fats is considered key to success in muscle building. However, the author stresses that caloric intake should be adjusted according to individual needs.

First and foremost, the text underscores the importance of functional training, which involves exercises that mimic common movements in daily life. This type of training has gained popularity as it engages multiple muscles simultaneously, leading to quicker muscle growth compared to other training methods. The author emphasizes that functional training is particularly useful for athletes looking to enhance their performance in specific physical activities.

Additionally, the "FROM GEEK TO FREAK" section describes the significance of proper hydration for improving physical performance. The author stresses how critical it is to keep the body well-hydrated during workouts to enhance endurance and overall health. Specifically, the author advises drinking plenty of water before, during, and after exercise to maintain hydration.

The section also focuses on the importance of injury prevention during training. The author highlights that certain weightlifting techniques can cause severe back, knee, or shoulder injuries. To avoid these injuries, the author recommends following proper lifting techniques, not overloading with excessive weights, and incorporating stretching before and after workouts.

Lastly, the "FROM GEEK TO FREAK" section offers guidance on making gradual and consistent improvements. The author emphasizes the importance of not pushing the body beyond its capabilities but rather following steady progressions in training load and intensity over time. Following these gradual progressions allows the body to adapt gradually to the training without the risk of injuries.

In summary, the "FROM GEEK TO FREAK" section provides a comprehensive overview of key aspects of muscle growth training, with insights into secondary topics like functional training, hydration, the importance of proper stretching and lifting techniques, and the significance of gradual training progression. It emphasizes the importance of rest and maintaining a balanced caloric intake for achieving the best results.

OCCAM'S PROTOCOL I

The subchapter "Occam's Protocol I" presents a comprehensive guide to a short yet highly intensive six-week training program designed to efficiently and quickly increase muscle mass and strength. This training program is based on multi-joint exercises performed with heavy weight loads.

The text underscores the importance of executing multi-joint exercises to increase the secretion of testosterone and growth hormones that promote muscle mass growth. In the program, each exercise is performed with such a high load that the subject can complete only 4 to 6 repetitions.

Occam's Protocol I dictates that each muscle group is trained only twice a week, in contrast to other training programs that might recommend training each muscle group once a week. The author emphasizes the importance of recovery time for training results, as it allows muscles to repair and grow.

The subchapter provides a detailed description of each multi-joint exercise included in the training program. Furthermore, guidelines on the number of repetitions, sets, and necessary rest periods to achieve maximum benefit from each exercise are provided. Different strategies for varying the loads during training are also illustrated.

Finally, the subchapter discusses the importance of proper and balanced nutrition to achieve optimal results from the training program. The author highlights that even though the actual exercise time required by the program is minimal (about 2-3 hours per week), following a diet tailored to the type of training is essential for success.

First and foremost, the text underscores the importance of weight training for overall body health. Weight training, according to the text, not only helps build muscle mass but also improves bone density, heart health, metabolic resistance, and sleep quality. Additionally, weight training is an excellent option for those looking to achieve results in less time compared to other activities like running or swimming.

The training program proposed in the text is also interesting because it can be performed at home or in the gym with simple equipment like barbells and dumbbells, without the need for expensive and complex equipment.

Another topic in this subchapter is the importance of avoiding overtraining, which means not pushing training to excessive extremes. The author emphasizes the importance of maintaining a good balance between training and rest to prevent potential injuries. Additionally, the subchapter provides some suggestions on proper nutrition to complement the training program.

The "Occam's Protocol I" subchapter also offers insightful information about muscle structure and the functioning of muscle fibers. It explains the differences between slow and fast-twitch muscle fibers and how high-intensity training can increase the size of fast-twitch muscle fibers.

Lastly, the subchapter provides advice on the use of dietary supplements to increase muscle growth and enhance the training program's performance. Recommended supplements include protein powder, branched-chain amino acids (BCAA), creatine, and glucose.

In summary, the "Occam's Protocol I" subchapter provides a comprehensive guide for building muscle mass and improving strength in a short time. In addition to the principles of the high-intensity training program, the text offers important information on the significance of nutrition, muscle structure, muscle fiber function, and the use of dietary supplements.

OCCAM'S PROTOCOL II

The subchapter called "OCCAM'S PROTOCOL II: The Finer Points" caters to those looking to up their fitness game beyond Protocol I. Here's a detailed breakdown of the main topics covered in the subchapter:

- Modified Protocol for Those Who Don't Meet Protocol I Requirements: Tim Ferriss, the book's author, has included an alternative protocol for newcomers to strength training, those with limited experience, or those who don't meet the physical requirements of Protocol I. This modified version involves bodyweight exercises like squats and push-ups, replacing free weights to prepare the body for strength training.

- In-Depth Workout Program Explanation: The subchapter provides an extensive explanation of the workout program, encompassing exercises, set and repetition numbers, rest periods, and cycle duration. A key point in this program is the use of compound exercises like deadlifts and squats, engaging multiple muscle groups, promoting balanced strength development. Other parts of the program include exercises targeting arm and core development and the incorporation of kettlebells for enhanced endurance.

- Emphasis on Recovery Between Sets and Exercises: Tim Ferriss underscores the importance of recovery between sets and exercises, which aids in maximizing muscle growth and preventing injuries. Adequate rest between sets should be at least 90 seconds, and the protocol also incorporates a full recovery day between training sessions.

- Muscle Growth Diet Program: The subchapter delves into the significance of nutrition in achieving muscle growth goals. Ferriss suggests adopting a diet rich in proteins, carbohydrates, and healthy fats to support muscle growth and aid in muscle repair post-workout. He provides an overview of the best sources for each essential nutrient required for muscle growth and recommends crafting a personalized diet to meet individual needs.

To sum it up, "OCCAM'S PROTOCOL II: The Finer Points" is a crucial subchapter in the book "Building the Perfect Posterior," offering a detailed overview of Tim Ferriss's training protocol designed for those aiming for advanced muscle growth goals. The program focuses on compound exercises, adequate rest between sets, and a personalized diet.

Additionally, here are the secondary topics covered within the subchapter:

- Time Under Tension Control: The subchapter emphasizes the importance of maintaining precise control of time under tension during exercises to maximize muscle growth. Ferriss recommends slow and controlled repetitions, with a 1-2 second contraction phase and a 3-4 second extension phase.

- Proper Breathing Technique: Proper breathing is a key element in any strength training program. Ferriss explains the significance of breathing correctly during exercises to ensure an adequate oxygen flow to the muscles. Specifically, he suggests inhaling during the descent phase (when the muscle lengthens) and exhaling during the ascent phase (when the muscle shortens).

- High Repetition Usage: Ferriss suggests incorporating high repetitions (less weight, more repetitions) as part of a comprehensive training program to improve muscular endurance. He advises using light weights (around 50% of your maximum) and performing 15-30 repetitions per set.

- Warm-Up and Stretching: The subchapter discusses the importance of warming up and stretching before a workout, which can help prevent injuries and enhance performance. Ferriss provides specific warm-up exercises for each body part, such as shoulder movements to prepare for deadlifts and static stretching to increase quad mobility.

- Calculating Percentage of Maximum: Using a percentage of your maximum (the maximum weight you can lift once) as a reference for training volume. By employing a percentage of the maximum, you can adjust training intensity, making progress easier to measure.

- Program Evaluation and Revision: To effectively assess your training program, Ferriss recommends using the cumulative effects method and recording progress over time to monitor strength and muscle mass increases. If necessary, the training protocol can be tailored based on individual performance and needs.

In short, "OCCAM'S PROTOCOL II: The Finer Points" within the book "Building the Perfect Posterior" also covers several critical secondary topics related to time under tension control, proper breathing, high repetition usage, warm-up and stretching, percentage of maximum calculations, and program evaluation and revision, all aimed at fostering continuous progress over time.

IMPROVING SEX

Reading Time: 3 mins 50 secs

"THE 15-MINUTE FEMALE ORGASM"

The "15-Minute Female Orgasm" chapter introduces a technique that requires unwavering focus on a specific area, sans any specific goal or pressure. It encourages 15 minutes of mindfulness in which the woman lies down, legs apart and feet together, all while concentrating on this zone. This technique doesn't entail full sexual acts and serves as a means to increase one's body awareness.

"THE 15-MINUTE FEMALE ORGASM- Part Deux"

In this chapter, the author delves into a technique designed to help women achieve orgasm. It involves 15-minute sessions where the partner solely uses their fingers, focusing on the clitoral area. The reader is instructed on how to apply this method and avoid common mistakes. Towards the end of the chapter, there's a brief discussion about stimulating the G-spot. The primary focus of the chapter remains on the 15-minute method for female orgasm.

"SEX MACHINE I"

The author's experience with heightened testosterone levels and the feelings of increased strength and stamina, akin to a superhero, is detailed in this chapter. He also shares insights into the "bed scratches" left by his partner and their surprisingly rapid healing. Essentially, the chapter delves into some of the author's experiences regarding his sexuality and hormonal system.

"HAPPY ENDINGS AND DOUBLING SPERM COUNT"

The chapter extensively explores the alarming decline in sperm counts worldwide, dissecting various factors affecting male fertility. Risk factors such as smoking, obesity, and stress are outlined as significant contributors to plummeting sperm counts. Furthermore, the author highlights how excessive heat, alcohol and drug consumption, poor diet, and exposure to harmful chemicals can significantly impact male fertility.

The chapter also delves into potential solutions. The author emphasizes the adoption of lifestyle changes and natural remedies to enhance male fertility and increase sperm counts. Strategies like incorporating natural supplements such as zinc and vitamin C, maintaining a healthy diet by avoiding processed foods, smoking, and toxins, as well as engaging in physical exercise to maintain a healthy weight, are elaborated upon.

Of particular interest in this chapter is the emotional toll male infertility can take on individuals. The author contends that infertility can negatively impact relationships and self-esteem, but also suggests that individuals can resolve this issue by seeking effective solutions to improve their overall health and well-being.

Let's delve deeper into the secondary aspects of the chapter titled "HAPPY ENDINGS AND DOUBLING SPERM COUNT."

1. Personal Experience: The author draws on their personal experience to underscore the importance of monitoring one's sperm count. Sharing their own journey of measuring sperm counts and identifying the causes of any issues emphasizes the need for proactive sexual health monitoring. The author highlights that addressing these issues proactively is crucial, as they are often underestimated.

2. Psychological Impact: The detrimental effects of male infertility on the lives of those affected by the issue deserve further exploration. The author underscores how depression, anxiety, and stress can significantly influence an individual's social and professional life. Additionally, the text stresses how discovering effective solutions to enhance male fertility can have a positive impact on an individual's mental health.

3. Age as a Risk Factor: The chapter discusses the role of advanced age as a risk factor for male fertility issues. Delving deeper into this aspect, the author emphasizes how age can negatively affect male reproductive function. The suggestion that individuals should consider their sexual health from a young age to prevent long-term reproductive problems can be expanded upon, perhaps by discussing the changing landscape of fertility awareness across generations.

4. Medical Solutions: While the text briefly touches on medical solutions such as hormone therapy, surgery, and in vitro fertilization, a more comprehensive discussion of these options is warranted. It's crucial to underline the importance of not relying solely on medical interventions and adopting a holistic approach to enhance one's sexual health and increase sperm counts.

In summary, "HAPPY ENDINGS AND DOUBLING SPERM COUNT" covers a range of interconnected topics related to male fertility, including declining sperm counts, natural remedies, lifestyle considerations, infertility prevention, the psychological impact of male infertility, age as a risk factor, and potential medical interventions. Further development of these aspects can provide readers with a more comprehensive understanding of the subject matter.

PERFECTING SLEEP

Reading Time: 4 mins 17 secs

ENGINEERING THE PERFECT NIGHT'S SLEEP

Subchapter "Engineering the Perfect Night's Sleep" offers valuable insights and practical advice on achieving a deeper, more restful, and regenerative sleep. Here are some of the key points covered in the document:

1. Sleep Analysis: The text emphasizes the importance of analyzing your sleep patterns to improve them, providing examples of useful tools such as the Sleep Cycle iPhone app and the Zeo device. These tools assist users in monitoring the quality of their sleep and identifying any issues.

2. Duration and Quality of REM Sleep: Another fundamental concept is the significance of REM sleep for the quality of rest and memory. The text highlights that sleep quality depends on the ratio of total sleep to REM sleep, rather than the absolute duration of REM sleep.

3. Huperzine A: The text also discusses the use of Huperzine A, an extract from Huperzia serrata, to increase the amount of REM sleep and describes how it slows down the degradation of the neurotransmitter acetylcholine. However, it is mentioned that excessive use of this extract can lead to side effects such as insomnia and interactions with certain categories of medications.

4. Lucid Dreaming: The author also delves into "lucid dreaming" and describes how it can be used to accelerate skill learning,

enhance sports performance, and reactivate "forgotten" languages. Furthermore, the use of Huperzine A to facilitate lucid dreaming is mentioned.

5. Other Contributions: The text outlines the contributions of other tools, such as humidifiers and smart alarm applications like WakeMate, to improve sleep quality. It also underscores the importance of diet and physical activity in enhancing sleep quality.

To conclude, the chapter "Engineering the Perfect Night's Sleep" provides in-depth information and diverse practical strategies for improving sleep quality. The techniques described in the text cover a wide range of topics, including sleep analysis, the duration and quality of REM sleep, the use of supplements like Huperzine A, the practice of lucid dreaming, and the contribution of other tools such as humidifiers and smart alarm applications. By implementing these techniques, users should be able to enhance sleep quality and enjoy better rest.

BECOMING UBERMAN

Let's explore "BECOMING UBERMAN," a chapter within "PERFECTING SLEEP," all about the intriguing concept of polyphasic sleep. It's all about sleeping less while achieving better performance through dividing your sleep into several chunks. The text delves into why people are drawn to this approach, like the potential for extra free time or enhanced daily performance.

Now, in the realm of polyphasic sleep, you encounter various sleep cycles: Uberman, Dymaxion, and Everyman. Uberman, the most extreme and challenging cycle, involves six 20-minute naps evenly spaced throughout the day. On the flip side, Dymaxion comprises four 30-minute naps, and Everyman combines a core sleep of roughly three to four hours with three 20-minute power naps.

One of the key perks of adopting a polyphasic sleep pattern is the ability to gain more waking hours without detrimental effects on cognitive and physical performance. This approach seems to optimize the balance between light and deep sleep, resulting in improved cognitive and physical capabilities.

But, like any unconventional approach, there are challenges and downsides. It takes a while to adapt to this fragmented sleep, which can affect your social life and daily activities.

In addition to the primary points, "BECOMING UBERMAN" explores some extra dimensions of polyphasic sleep.

The primary motivation behind this sleep cycle is the promise of more free time and heightened daytime performance. Beyond that, there are other benefits, such as easier adjustment to different time zones, enhanced blood circulation, and a reduced risk of heart diseases.

The chapter also uncovers some specific sleep cycles, with Uberman standing out as the most demanding to adhere to consistently but offering the most significant benefits in terms of cognitive and physical performance.

Moreover, it highlights potential difficulties in adopting polyphasic sleep. There could be challenges in sleeping in fragmented segments during the day, which might impact sleep quality and social interactions. And let's not forget, maintaining this sleep regimen requires discipline, demanding a more significant physical and mental effort compared to traditional sleep.

In summary, the text suggests that polyphasic sleep has the potential to enhance performance and promote more efficient rest. However, it's not a one-size-fits-all solution and calls for a dedicated commitment to follow through consistently. And, if you're considering this approach, consulting a sleep specialist is always a smart move.

In conclusion, "BECOMING UBERMAN" sheds light on the possibilities and limitations of polyphasic sleep, offering insights and tips for those intrigued by the idea. It might pique the interest of folks aiming to maximize their performance, with the promise of extra waking hours without compromising cognitive and physical abilities.

REVERSING INJURIES

Reading Time: 7 mins 21 secs

REVERSING "PERMANENT" INJURIES

Let's delve into "REVERSING 'PERMANENT' INJURIES," a chapter that uncovers the author's journey in attempting to reverse the effects of what seemed like irreparable physical injuries. The author lays out a multi-stage approach aimed at gradually resolving these physical challenges.

Central to this approach is a focus on correcting posture and body movement. It's argued that one of the primary contributors to physical discomfort is poor posture and inefficient movement. The author asserts that addressing these aspects can be a highly effective means of alleviating these symptoms. For instance, ditching heeled shoes and opting for Vibram footwear is cited as a successful tactic in reducing lower back pain.

The author also finds success in the Egoscue Method, a postural exercise methodology designed to rectify issues through specific exercises. In the text, the Egoscue Method is credited with helping resolve physical problems, especially those linked to back posture.

Crucially, the text underscores that the list of treatments and methodologies employed is just one example of what's possible. Each case may require a unique, personalized approach.

What sets this chapter apart is the deeply personal narrative. It encompasses the tough moments, setbacks, and positive developments within the author's healing journey. This personal account serves to paint a realistic and practical picture of the path one might undertake when seeking to reverse seemingly permanent physical injuries.

In essence, "REVERSING 'PERMANENT' INJURIES" provides an overview of methodologies and treatments used by the author to overcome physical injuries and alleviate physical discomfort. The primary topics here are posture and body movement correction, the use of specific footwear like Vibram shoes, the Egoscue Method, and the author's personal experiences within the healing journey.

But there's more to explore in this chapter, including secondary subjects:

Firstly, it emphasizes the importance of targeted physical exercise for injury resolution. The author describes adopting a gradual approach to exercise, slowly increasing physical activity to a suitable level without causing further harm. Targeted physical exercise can be effective in improving muscle functionality and preventing future issues.

Secondly, it discusses the role of stretching and mobilization exercises in healing muscle discomfort. The text explains how these exercises can be used in conjunction with other methods to facilitate the resolution of specific issues, such as Achilles tendon inflammation.

Another key point revolves around the use of specific dietary supplements. The author mentions that taking collagen supplements and other products aimed at muscle health can aid the healing process. However, it's also stressed that product quality should be closely monitored, and consulting a healthcare professional before starting any supplement regimen is essential.

Moreover, the chapter provides detailed information on the use of manual therapy, such as therapeutic massage, which can be effective in reducing muscle tension and enhancing blood circulation. The author describes how massage and other forms of manual therapy have been used in combination with other methods to reduce pain and improve physical functionality.

In summary, the chapter "REVERSING 'PERMANENT' INJURIES" explores various secondary topics that can be valuable in reversing seemingly permanent physical injuries and resolving muscle discomfort. These include the importance of safe and targeted physical exercise, the need for stretching and mobilization, the use of specific dietary supplements, and the utilization of manual therapy.

HOW TO PAY FOR A BEACH VACATION WITH ONE HOSPITAL VISIT

The document at hand delves into the intriguing world of injury reversal, employing unconventional strategies for recovering one's health, exploring cellular health, and enhancing performance through the use of chemicals and other therapies.

1.*Injury Reversal:
This text focuses on the intriguing possibility of reversing so-called "permanent" injuries through the use of unconventional techniques and methodologies. It introduces prolotherapy, an injection technique designed to stimulate the body's repair system. This method temporarily triggers an inflammatory response to activate the healing process in damaged tissues. Furthermore, it mentions the concept of tensegrity, a theory suggesting that the human body is a support system composed of soft and bony

tissues. This idea underpins various approaches for addressing musculoskeletal and postural issues, such as the Egoscue therapy.

2. Unconventional Healing Experiences:
The text weaves a captivating narrative about the author's unusual experiences in healing certain injuries. It recounts an experimental treatment involving larvae for a skin infection, conducted in Mexico. Additionally, it explores the use of unconventional medical treatments as alternatives to traditional therapies for ailments or injuries that don't respond to conventional methods.

3. Cellular Health:
This text also delves into the optimization of cellular health to enhance athletic or cognitive performance. It introduces the concept of nootropics, substances used to boost cognitive performance and creative thinking. The text also explores theories related to the creation and use of personalized medications that can adapt to the individual needs of each patient.

4. Tools and Hacks:
The text provides various tools and tricks to assist individuals in improving their health and preventing injuries. These include the Functional Movement Screen (FMS), an assessment used to identify muscular imbalances and movement dysfunctions, as well as explanatory videos on how to correctly perform exercises like Squats, Turkish Get-Ups (TGU), and Cross-body One-arm Single-leg deadlifts.

In conclusion, the text primarily focuses on unconventional techniques and methodologies for injury treatment, showcases exemplary healing stories, and explores the use of chemicals and therapies to enhance cellular health. While these approaches may appear unconventional, they are indeed intriguing options to consider when addressing certain health issues.

PRE-HAB

The subchapter "PRE-HAB" primarily focuses on injury prevention through pre-habilitation techniques and its significance in effective training. It underscores the importance of injury prevention in the context of physical fitness and sports training. Injuries can be significant roadblocks to achieving fitness goals and can cause considerable discomfort and pain. To address this, the author suggests the adoption of pre-hab techniques. These techniques encompass exercises and habits aimed at preventing injuries rather than treating them. This approach maximizes performance and minimizes the risk of injuries.

Additionally, the text emphasizes the importance of pre-habilitation for effective and safe training, especially in high-impact or contact sports. Paying special attention to joint and muscle preparation is essential. This involves adopting exercises for mobilization, stabilization, and strengthening to prevent injuries and muscle pains. This helps maximize training effectiveness and accelerates recovery.

The subchapter suggests the use of specific exercises like dynamic stretching, joint warm-ups, and muscle strengthening to prevent injuries and improve athletic performance. The text also identifies less effective exercises and risky movements, such as knee flexion or stepping back, which can increase the risk of injuries.

The author also provides a personal account of the importance of stretching in their athletic experience. A proper stretching routine has been instrumental in preventing injuries and enhancing overall physical performance.

Furthermore, the text details several exercises useful for muscle and joint development, such as the Cross-Body One-Arm Single-

Leg Deadlift, Squat, and Turkish Get-Up. It also highlights exercises that pose a risk of injury, such as squatting with inward knee movement or combining weight lifting with stepping back.

The text introduces various tools for physical training, including the Metolius Nylon Daisy Chain for C&L, the Black Diamond HotWire Carabiner for C&L, and Kayaking Dry Bags. These tools can contribute to a more comprehensive and correct training regimen.

The author suggests adopting a two-week weekly training program with a coordination phase in the first week using light movements to correct motor skills, followed by a testing phase in the second week to identify and correct any pre-existing muscle imbalances.

The subchapter also emphasizes the importance of flexibility training and muscle balance through specific exercises like joint warm-ups, dynamic stretching, and mobilization. The goal is to adequately prepare the body for physical activity and make it more efficient in movement.

Lastly, the text describes the need to pay attention to joint preparation to increase training effectiveness and reduce the risk of injuries. It offers valuable advice on strengthening the musculoskeletal system through pre-hab techniques and the correct execution of specific exercises.

The subchapter "PRE-HAB"- REVERSING INJURIES" provides valuable insights into adopting pre-habilitation techniques and habits for injury prevention, both in basic training and for high-impact sports.

RUNNING FASTER AND FARTHER

Reading Time: 9 mins 21 secs

HACKING THE NFL COMBINE I

The primary topics of the subchapter titled "HACKING THE NFL COMBINE I."
1. Importance of Measurables in the NFL Scouting Combine:
   - The subchapter highlights the significance of physical tests known as "measurables" in the player selection process of American football within the NFL Scouting Combine. These tests are crucial for assessing athletes' physical abilities, including speed, strength, and agility, aiding recruiters in evaluating if these abilities align with their team's requirements.

2. Joe DeFranco's Innovative Technique - "Hacking the Three-Cone Drill":
   - The subchapter introduces Joe DeFranco, an athletic coach who developed an alternative technique known as "Hacking the Three-Cone Drill." DeFranco's method has demonstrated the ability to produce better results for athletes during the NFL Scouting Combine tests when compared to traditional approaches. This method serves to improve the performance of athletes specifically in the three-cone drill.

3. Pragmatic Equipment Choices in Joe DeFranco's Gym:*
   - The text discusses the selection of equipment in Joe DeFranco's gym, emphasizing efficiency and utility over popularity. This approach ensures that the equipment used maximizes its value, enabling athletes to engage in effective training to achieve optimal results.

Secondary Topics Mentioned in the Subchapter:

4. Dave Tate's Influence on Sumo Deadlift Technique:
   - The subchapter mentions the influence of Dave Tate, a powerlifting icon, who advised positioning the hips as close to the barbell as possible during the execution of the sumo deadlift. This technique compels the muscles in the pelvis to work more, potentially enhancing an athlete's performance in various exercises, including the three-cone drill. It can also improve the execution speed by reducing the distance the athlete's legs need to cover, which, in turn, reduces transition time and enhances the fluidity of the movement.

5. Mental Preparation and Stress Management:
   - The text underscores that the NFL Scouting Combine is one of the most stressful situations for an athlete as it can determine their future career in American football. Therefore, adequate athlete preparation is crucial, focusing on developing the right mentality and motivation to improve their confidence during the tests. Techniques such as visualization and controlled breathing are used by Joe DeFranco to help athletes stay calm and focused during the physical tests.

6. Specific Training Methods for the NFL Scouting Combine:
   - The subchapter emphasizes the importance of using specific training methods to prepare for the NFL Scouting Combine. For instance, specific exercises for the three-cone drill may involve the use of cones to enhance an athlete's ability to change direction quickly and accelerate. Additionally, proprioceptive training methods simulate specific game actions and focus on creating a strong connection between an athlete's nervous and muscular systems.

To concluse, the subchapter "HACKING THE NFL COMBINE I" in the chapter "RUNNING FASTER AND FARTHER" provides comprehensive information on both the primary and secondary topics. The main subjects include the importance of measurables in the NFL Scouting Combine, innovative techniques like Joe DeFranco's "Hacking the Three-Cone Drill," and pragmatic equipment choices in DeFranco's gym. Secondary topics encompass the influence of Dave Tate's technique, mental preparation, and specific training methods to excel in the NFL Scouting Combine.

HACKING THE NFL COMBINE II

"HACKING THE NFL COMBINE II" highlights the critical role of physical measurements in the selection process of NFL draft players. The author underscores how metrics like speed, vertical jump, and strength significantly influence the choices made by NFL teams during the draft.

In this section, we dive into the significance of these physical measurements in the NFL draft process. These metrics, including sprint speed, vertical jump ability, and strength, are pivotal factors that shape the decisions of NFL teams when selecting new players.

To elevate the performance of aspiring NFL players during the draft, we meet Joe DeFranco, a trainer on a mission. His goal is to fine-tune players for the NFL Combine, an annual event where NFL teams scrutinize the physical capabilities of potential new recruits. DeFranco employs advanced, customized training techniques to help these players sharpen their skills.

The text also delves into running technique, emphasizing the importance of body posture and the "Pose Method." This technique leverages gravity to propel movement, advocates landing on the heels rather than the toes, maintaining a slight leg bend, and exercising control over one's pace. Notably, this running technique endorsed by renowned athletes and coaches was originally developed by Russian physicist and university professor Nicolas S. Romanov PhD.

Finally, the text underscores the value of video analysis for evaluating and enhancing running technique. Video analysis serves as a powerful tool for identifying and correcting improper body positioning and flawed running techniques. When coupled with advanced training methods, video analysis becomes a potent means of optimizing the performance of football players.

On a related note, a secondary theme addressed by the author is the importance of maintaining good posture to boost performance in American football. It's highlighted that maintaining the right balance and posture, including a straight back, is instrumental in achieving maximum strength and physical stability during activities such as running, jumping, and the various maneuvers characteristic of football.

Shifting our focus to the second major point, the text underscores the role of advanced equipment and technology in enhancing the performance of football players. It provides examples like the use of elastic resistance bands, which contribute to strengthening the lower body. Moreover, fitness monitoring devices are lauded for assisting football players in setting and tracking their training goals, thereby enhancing the efficiency of their fitness journey.

Furthermore, the text places significant emphasis on the importance of nutrition for improving football player performance. It stresses the value of a balanced diet that incorporates proteins, complex carbohydrates, and healthy fats, providing the necessary energy for players to tackle demanding workouts and games. Simultaneously, it emphasizes the need to avoid junk food, sugary beverages, and to maintain a balanced diet.

Last but not least, the text touches upon the significance of mental resilience for football players. It's not just about physical fitness and a balanced diet; mental fortitude is just as vital when confronting the challenges in football, be it injuries, losses, or pain.

In summary, "HACKING THE NFL COMBINE II" within the text dives deep into the importance of physical measurements for NFL players and the work of Joe DeFranco in preparing them for the NFL Combine. We also explore running techniques, the utilization of video analysis, maintaining proper posture, harnessing advanced equipment and technology, the critical role of nutrition, and the mental strength required in the game of football.

ULTRAENDURANCE I

In the chapter "ULTRAENDURANCE I" of the book "Running Faster and Farther," several topics related to athletic training and performance enhancement are discussed. In addition to the main points mentioned earlier, there are secondary aspects that contribute to the overall understanding of the chapter.

A significant point concerns joint mobility. The importance of exercises aimed at improving flexibility and the ability to perform correct movements is emphasized. Good joint mobility not only reduces the risk of injuries but also enhances the quality of movement during physical activity, thereby contributing to improved performance.

The chapter also outlines the approach of high-intensity training known as "metabolic conditioning," which aims to enhance athletic endurance through high-intensity exercises.

Furthermore, the text provides valuable insights into how the use of whey protein supplements can be helpful in developing and maintaining muscle after intense physical activity.

Addressing the importance of rest, it highlights the significance of good sleep quality for energy recovery and the long-term maintenance of sports performance. In this regard, establishing habits that promote proper sleep quality becomes essential.

Lastly, the chapter offers an overview of running as a teachable skill through the concepts presented in the book "Pose Method," providing practical advice on improving running technique.

To conclude, the chapter "ULTRAENDURANCE I" in the book "Running Faster and Farther" provides a comprehensive overview of aspects related to athletic training, running, and the use of specific exercises and supplements to enhance sports performance. The text offers a detailed analysis of various aspects, providing readers with in-depth knowledge of practical tools to improve their performance, provided that it is supported by proper nutrition and appropriate training periodization.

ULTRAENDURANCE II

In the chapter "ULTRAENDURANCE II," we're diving deep into the physical preparation needed to go from a 5 km run to conquering a 50 km race in just 12 weeks. One of the key takeaways is understanding the limitations of the human body: our liver and muscles can only store a limited amount of carbohydrates. When running becomes anaerobic, meaning without oxygen, the body has to dip into these limited reserves. This can lead to early fatigue and a drop in performance.

To illustrate this challenge, the text shares the story of a 43-year-old woman who couldn't improve her running speed because she quickly went anaerobic. This was due to her body's inefficient use of oxygen during the run. To overcome this limitation, the text suggests following a gradual training program that allows the body to adapt progressively to long-distance running.

Furthermore, the chapter emphasizes the significance of proper nutrition to support training and enhance performance. Specifically, it's pointed out that the liver and muscles can only store a certain amount of carbohydrates. Therefore, it's important to consume complex carbohydrates and proteins to sustain your training and aid muscle recovery. Additionally, the text highlights the importance of staying adequately hydrated during both training and the actual race. Avoiding heavy, fatty foods before running is also advised.

Next, in the "ULTRAENDURANCE II" section, the text underscores the importance of proper running technique to improve performance and prevent injuries. Focus is placed on posture, step cadence, and breathing during the run. High step cadence, meaning the number of steps per minute, is particularly emphasized to enhance running efficiency and reduce the risk of injuries. Landing on the midfoot instead of the heel, keeping your knees slightly bent, and maintaining an upright posture during the run are all recommended techniques. Additionally, the text stresses the importance of proper breathing while running, with deep inhalations and regular exhalations to ensure your muscles receive an adequate oxygen supply. By following these techniques, you can enhance your running form and reduce the risk of injuries during training and races.

GETTING STRONGER

Reading Time: 4 mins 56 secs

EFFORTLESS SUPERHUMAN

The "EFFORTLESS SUPERHUMAN" subchapter kicks off by introducing Barry Ross and his unconventional training approach that has revolutionized athletics. Ross's training method focuses on increasing ground support forces rather than cutting down running times or enhancing leg movement.

The following paragraph dives into Barry Ross's successful training of the athlete Allyson Felix. Ross's training protocol for Felix includes a thrice-weekly workout regimen, starting with dynamic stretching. Afterward, athletes have the option of resistance exercises, choosing between flat bench presses and push-ups. Next up is conventional deadlifting with a barbell, never surpassing knee height. Participants are also taught to drop the barbell rather than lowering it slowly to avoid the eccentric phase and reduce the risk of hamstring muscle injuries.

Once these two phases are complete, athletes perform plyometric exercises (varying height box jumps) for 4-6 reps before moving on to core exercises, including isometric and core control workouts. The training session wraps up with a session of static stretching.

The text then delves into the scientific foundations of Barry Ross's method. Research demonstrates that the greater the ground support force, the higher an athlete's top speed can be. Felix has been specifically trained to enhance the support force in each leg to boost her sprint. Barry Ross's training is grounded in science and biomechanics to help athletes achieve exceptional performance.

The author continues by explaining that the bent-knee deadlift is one of the critical exercises in Ross's program. It's a core strength exercise involving the back, legs, forearms, and arms. Ross recommends performing the exercise with 85-95% of one's one-repetition maximum, maintaining proper technique to prevent injuries.

The text proceeds to discuss the use of accessories like Fat Gripz to improve grip strength. Fat Gripz are grip training tools that can be applied to standard barbells, allowing athletes to train grip-related muscles. Ross suggests using these accessories occasionally, alternating between lighter and heavier weights.

Lastly, the chapter outlines strategies to enhance the three power lifts: bench press, squat, and deadlift. Jim Wendler, the guide's author, offers an alternative to the commonly used five-rep max (5RM) protocol. Wendler suggests focusing on 85% of one's one-repetition max for better long-term results.

In conclusion, in the "EFFORTLESS SUPERHUMAN" protocol, Barry Ross presents an innovative training approach that is redefining the standards of track and field. His method is centered on improving ground support forces to enable athletes to reach their maximum speeds. The training protocol encompasses dynamic stretching, resistance exercises, bent-knee deadlifts, core plyometric exercises, and static stretching. This method has proven successful with athlete Allyson Felix and continues to be a winning methodology for athletes worldwide.

EATING THE ELEPHANT

The "EATING THE ELEPHANT" subchapter in "GETTING STRONGER" focuses on improving bench press performance, aiming to provide readers with tips and tricks to surpass their limits. Firstly, it emphasizes the importance of setting specific and motivating goals, highlighting that motivation is the key to success in any field, including sports training.

The text also offers various examples of high-level weightlifting and powerlifting athletes, such as Mark Bell and Jeremy Frey, citing their experiences and training techniques to inspire readers to enhance their bench press performance. Additionally, the book underscores how the experience of a good coach can make a significant difference in achieving great results.

The chapter goes on to discuss the theme of recovery, defining it as an essential element of an effective training program. It emphasizes that if not taken seriously, it can easily lead to overtraining. For this reason, the text also provides several recovery strategies that will help readers avoid this issue.

In addition to the main points described in my previous response, the "EATING THE ELEPHANT" subchapter in the "GETTING STRONGER" chapter also presents a number of secondary topics that are useful for a full understanding of the text's content.

First, it underscores the importance of proper caloric intake and nutrition for training success. The goal is to build muscle mass and reduce body fat, thereby enhancing sports performance. The book recommends following a suitable diet and provides valuable information on the significance of macros and micronutrients.

A second fascinating topic is the analysis of the nervous system in weight training. The text suggests how to optimize one's nervous system for the best bench press results, for example, through neuromuscular system sensitization and the utilization of "hyperclocking" the nervous system.

There are also some specific techniques for increasing muscle strength, such as the use of isokinetic machines and the "grease the groove" technique, which focuses on training the ability to perform exercises repetitively while gradually increasing exercise intensity.

Another notable topic is the importance of posture during exercise execution. Good posture is crucial for preventing physical issues and ensuring the effectiveness of training. The book provides numerous examples of specific exercises to improve posture and make the most of the spine's correct alignment.

Finally, the text focuses on the importance of sleep for muscle recovery. Quality sleep is fundamental for improving sports performance, and the text offers some advice for enhancing the quality of rest, such as maintaining a regular circadian rhythm and appropriately managing body temperature. The book also lists several useful sources for those interested in delving further into sports training, such as Marty Gallagher's "The Purposeful Primitive" and "Powerlifting USA" magazine. Additionally, it provides links to interviews conducted by Tim Ferriss with top powerlifting athletes like Dave Tate, Jason Ferruggia, and Mike Robertson.

FROM SWIMMING TO SWINGING

Reading Time: 7 mins 55 secs

HOW I LEARNED TO SWIM EFFORTLESSLY IN 10 DAYS

The subchapter "HOW I LEARNED TO SWIM EFFORTLESSLY IN 10 DAYS" in the text "FROM SWIMMING TO SWINGING" narrates the author's struggles in learning how to swim and the method that eventually improved their skills. The author met Chris Sacca, a well-known triathlete and former Google employee, who introduced them to the Total Immersion (TI) learning method developed by American coach Terry Laughlin.

The Total Immersion method taught the author to swim more efficiently, with minimal effort, and without experiencing panic or stress in the water. The author describes in detail how the TI method drastically reduced water friction and resistance, enabling them to easily swim thirty pool lengths, compared to only four they could manage previously.

According to the author, a key to the success of the TI method lies in minimizing unnecessary movements, focusing on subtle actions like shoulder rotation and maintaining a horizontal body position. The author also emphasizes the importance of using the legs solely as a rudder, positioning the body for reduced water resistance.

To master this method, the author suggests watching the Total Immersion course DVD and reading the accompanying book, which provide step-by-step instructions on the required techniques.

The subchapter also offers eight tips for novice swimmers. The first piece of advice is to aim for maximum efficiency in the water, learning to move the body with minimal effort. The second tip is to keep the body horizontal, aligning the head with the spine and using the legs solely as a rudder, avoiding arm pulling or surface swimming. The third tip encourages alternating sides while swimming, instead of the typical face-down technique.

The remaining tips focus on speed, breathing, and mobility. The author advises increasing swimming speed by working on the stroke's frequency and suggests adopting breathing techniques, such as lateral breathing or the valve breath, which offer increased comfort during swimming. Finally, the author recommends doing mobility exercises to enhance range of motion and reduce the risk of injuries.

"HOW I LEARNED TO SWIM EFFORTLESSLY IN 10 DAYS" subchapter offers a comprehensive and engaging narrative of how the author learned to swim more efficiently and swiftly using the Total Immersion (TI) method. It also provides valuable advice for beginners looking to improve their water skills.

One key theme addresses the author's past challenges, which had hindered their swimming experience, having learned to swim later than their peers and struggling with the process.

The subchapter also delves into the concepts of "klappa" and "catch," which are crucial to mastering the TI method. "Klappa" refers to the use of hands as paddles to push water downward, aiding in movement. "Catch" relates to the ideal arm positioning in the water, contributing to enhanced propulsion.

Furthermore, the subchapter offers practical guidance on swimming instructors, recommending the search for well-trained and qualified professionals to work with. It also underscores the importance of maintaining a positive **mindset** during the learning and practice of swimming to achieve **better** results.

In conclusion, the "HOW I LEARNED TO SWIM EFFORTLESSLY IN 10 DAYS" subchapter not only focuses **on the** TI method for efficient swimming learning but also provides **valuable** secondary concepts such as the author's challenge in **learning** to swim, the "klappa" and "catch" concepts, advice on **swimming** instructors, and the importance of a positive mindset **during** practice. It serves as a comprehensive and valuable source of information for those seeking to improve their swimming **skills**.

THE ARCHITECTURE OF BABE RUTH

In the subchapter titled "THE ARCHITECTURE OF BABE RUTH," found in Chapter 12 of the book "FROM SWIMMING TO SWINGING," various insights about baseball and how a batter can strive to improve their stats are presented.

The author introduces the experience of Jaime Cevallos, a professional baseball coach who developed an innovative method for boosting players' performance. Cevallos utilizes a set of techniques based on the concept of CSR, which stands for "Connection, Speed, and Rotation."

The text goes on to explain that Slugging percentage is one of the primary performance metrics for batters in baseball. This metric reveals how well a player can hit for power and is considered one of the most indicative measures of success when assessing a baseball player's abilities.

Another key point of the subchapter concerns Babe Ruth's "Slot" position. Babe Ruth, a baseball legend, is known for his extraordinary hitting skills, and his "Slot" position is a crucial element that enabled him to be so effective.

Finally, one of the most successful techniques for improving batting ability is described as using the front hip's force to shift weight towards the opponent and hit the ball to the opposite field. However, it's emphasized that while this technique is highly effective, it can lead to significant soreness the following day.

In general, "THE ARCHITECTURE OF BABE RUTH" subchapter offers a detailed analysis of the factors contributing to baseball players' performance and the techniques that can be employed to enhance their batting abilities.

There are also some secondary topics of interest in this subchapter:

- The concept of AOI (Area of Impact) is described, highlighting how a larger area of impact can increase the power of the hit. This technique can be developed by improving hand and foot positioning.

- The text mentions an training method called the Impact Bag Drill, used by players to refine their batting technique. In this description, the importance of hitting a specific target is emphasized to develop a more precise and secure batting technique.

- The MP30 Training Bat is introduced as a tool to help batters establish the correct hand position during their batting technique. This equipment assists players in achieving an authoritative position over the ball during pitching, enhancing accuracy and power.

- The subchapter mentions the book "Moneyball: The Art of Winning an Unfair Game" by Michael Lewis, which details how the

Oakland Athletics achieved remarkable success in 2002 despite having the lowest salary in Major League Baseball. The text recounts how manager Billy Beane employed statistical analysis to acquire undervalued players in the market and how this led the Oakland Athletics to victory.

- The subchapter also describes the story of Jaime Cevallos, a professional baseball coach who created his innovative method to improve players' statistics. Thanks to his expertise and skills, many Major League Baseball players chose him as their personal coach, including some of the most famous baseball players who reached the pinnacle of their careers through his training techniques.

HOW TO HOLD YOUR BREATH LONGER THAN HOUDINI

The subchapter "HOW TO HOLD YOUR BREATH LONGER THAN HOUDINI," from the chapter "FROM SWIMMING TO SWINGING," focuses on the story of David Blaine, the famous magician and street artist, in his attempts to break the world record for assisted static apnea. The subchapter begins with a description of the challenge Blaine decided to take on: attempting to hold his breath for more than 17 minutes, surpassing the previous record. It discusses his numerous efforts to improve his breath-holding ability, including the idea of inserting a tube through his throat to breathe before submersion, an idea eventually rejected by Guinness World Record officials.

The subchapter particularly highlights Blaine's final attempt to break the record, which was successful, setting a new world record of 17 minutes and 4 seconds of assisted static apnea. It describes the moment when Blaine successfully broke the record and his reaction of disbelief and joy.

Additionally, the subchapter also describes training courses organized by Blaine to teach people how to improve their breath-holding capacity. Participants in a medical conference received specific training to learn how to hold their breath for longer periods and enhance their endurance. What the participants learned included how to regulate their breathing before submersion, how to relax during the dive, and how to manage anxiety and fear during the practice.

The subchapter provides an insight into the physiology of breathing and the effects of breath-holding on the body. For example, it describes how oxygen is rapidly consumed during a breath-holding test and how carbon dioxide significantly increases in the blood. It is also mentioned how prolonged exposure to hypoxia can lead to important physiological effects, such as the production of erythropoietin, which has beneficial effects on the body's physical capabilities.

Finally, the subchapter expands on the topic, focusing more broadly on how training in assisted static apnea and other mental and physical practices, like meditation and visualization, are part of a range of methodologies used to develop the physical and mental abilities of athletes. In this way, the subchapter offers a comprehensive and articulated view of how apnea is a valuable practice for improving physical endurance and the health of athletes and other specialists.

ON LONGER AND BETTER LIFE

Reading Time: 2 mins 33 secs

LIVING FOREVER

The chapter "ON LONGER AND BETTER LIFE" of the book discusses the topic of extended lifespan and how one can increase their longevity without compromising the quality of life.

At the beginning of the chapter, there is a discussion of a scientific experiment that highlights how a low-calorie diet can positively impact longevity, as demonstrated in an experiment involving monkeys. However, the author cautions against living a life of constant deprivation that might compromise the quality of life in the pursuit of longevity.

In connection with this theme, the author mentions several factors that can influence longevity, such as sexual activity in men. Specifically, a study is cited that suggests frequent male ejaculation may reduce the risk of prostate cancer. Additionally, moderate alcohol consumption is mentioned as a factor related to a longer life, citing a study from the University of Texas.

Throughout the chapter, the author discusses tools and strategies for leading a better life. It emphasizes the importance of living without continuous denials and deprivations. For example, the author encourages indulging in an occasional chocolate treat or engaging in regular and moderate sexual activity as ways to maintain one's mental and physical well-being while promoting longevity.

All these topics are presented in simple and accessible language, without the use of technical or scientific terms that might be difficult to understand. The subchapter also relates to the book "DRINKING GAMES: A memoir of the twenties gone wild" and offers an original and practical reflection on the importance of living a long and healthy life.

Furthermore, the author provides some tools and tips to promote longevity and quality of life. One such suggestion is blood donation, as the author recommends it as a way to lower iron levels in the blood and reduce the risk of diseases associated with iron buildup in the body.

The subchapter also mentions a cryonics facility called Alcor, where individuals can opt to have their bodies preserved through cryogenic suspension in case of terminal illness or death. According to the author, this could potentially allow individuals to be "awakened" in the future when medical science has made significant advancements.

The book "Transcend: Nine Steps to Living Well Forever" by Ray Kurzweil is also cited, which proposes nine strategies for extending life, including the use of genetic therapy and nanorobotics to repair damaged cells.

Lastly, the subchapter addresses the theme of laughter and humor. The author contends that laughter and amazement can extend one's life and cites an example of a study involving women with coronary artery disease who watched a comedy film and experienced improvements in coronary arteries in 22% of cases. This leads the author to recommend not being overly serious in life and not encroaching on the lives of social and group activities.

CLOSING THOUGHTS

Reading Time: 2 mins 46 secs

In the "CLOSING THOUGHTS", the author delves into the powerful link between physical fitness and mental strength. The key takeaway is that pushing the limits of endurance can have a remarkable impact on both your physical and mental well-being.

The chapter highlights how endurance training can instill a remarkable level of determination, transferring the mental toughness developed during long runs to various aspects of life. Engaging in physical activity, whether endurance sports or other forms of exercise, not only strengthens your body but can foster personal growth and a profound connection with your own physical self, partly due to the chemical responses triggered by training.

Additionally, the author introduces the concept of "transfer," where the physical conditioning achieved through one activity can be applied to excel in other areas of life. This is shown to boost self-esteem and confidence, making individuals more productive in their professional and personal lives.

One of the most compelling anecdotes in this chapter centers on the author's father. He embarked on a journey of weight loss and strength gain through physical activity, which significantly bolstered his self-confidence and earned him newfound respect from others. It underscores the idea that fitness can transform not only your body but also your social standing and how others perceive you.

In essence, the chapter underlines the profound connection between body and mind and how physical activity can enhance both aspects of our lives. It emphasizes the importance of maintaining physical health to improve mental well-being, providing a comprehensive perspective on how endurance training and general physical fitness can equip us with the tools to overcome hardships and tackle complex challenges.

The author touches on several secondary topics worth exploring. Firstly, the author highlights that endurance training is essentially structured stress for the body. This type of stress not only nurtures physical growth but also fosters mental resilience, preparing individuals to confront life's challenges with increased courage.

Another notable theme briefly touched upon is "MovNat." This training approach centers on replicating the primal movements our ancestors employed for survival. MovNat, which mimics actions like running, lifting, carrying, and climbing, offers a refreshing alternative to traditional exercise. It significantly contributes to enhanced physical and mental health, encompassing benefits such as increased strength, endurance, and flexibility.

The subchapter further delves into the importance of finding a training regimen that suits your individual characteristics and striking the right balance between pushing your boundaries and respecting your limits. Additionally, it highlights the significance of maintaining equilibrium between body and mind throughout your exercise routine and how this can positively influence your social and professional life.

In conclusion, the "CLOSING THOUGHTS" subchapter thoroughly explores various secondary themes, emphasizing the personal growth achieved through challenges, the value of training like our primal ancestors, the selection of a training regimen aligning with your unique qualities, the equilibrium between body and mind in exercise, and the subsequent enhancement of social and professional aspects of life. These elements deepen our understanding of the intricate link between body and mind, reinforcing their interdependence.

APPENDICES AND EXTRAS

Reading Time: 18 mins 37 secs

GETTING TESTED—FROM NUTRIENTS TO MUSCLE FIBERS

The main topic of the subchapter titled "GETTING TESTED—FROM NUTRIENTS TO MUSCLE FIBERS" revolves around the various types of tests that can be employed to assess one's body, spanning from blood tests to analyses of body composition. This subchapter also offers guidance on how to interpret test results wisely and not overly stress about tests that may not be pertinent or for which specific actions cannot be taken.

The goal of this subchapter is to emphasize the significance of tests in comprehending one's physical health better. It delves into different types of tests, including blood tests, body composition analyses, metabolic evaluations, and physical performance assessments. The author underscores how these tests can aid in identifying potential health issues or bodily dysfunctions, as well as recognizing one's strengths and weaknesses.

Furthermore, the author provides valuable insights into properly interpreting test results. It's pointed out that some individuals might be tempted to panic upon receiving test results indicating potential health problems. The key here is to accurately comprehend the results, interpret them suitably, and then take the necessary steps to address any identified issues.

Lastly, the author advises giving particular attention to test results that are relevant for long-term health and not overly stressing about tests that lack significance or for which no specific actions can be taken. In essence, focusing on results pertinent to long-term health can guide individuals toward a wellness strategy and overall health improvement.

In summary, the subchapter "GETTING TESTED - FROM NUTRIENTS TO MUSCLE FIBERS" provides essential counsel and suggestions to help individuals gain a better understanding of their test results and how to utilize them for long-term health enhancement. The author underscores the importance of avoiding unnecessary panic over test results and concentrating on tests relevant to overall health.

THE VALUE OF SELF EXPERIMENTATION

In the subchapter titled "THE VALUE OF SELF EXPERIMENTATION," the text underscores that self-experimentation can be an effective method for gaining new insights about oneself and conducting personal research. The primary focus lies in personalized learning and enhancing individual habits through self-directed experimentation. However, the text also acknowledges several limitations and challenges that one might encounter when embarking on self-experimentation. Notably, the high variability of results and the difficulty of controlling experimental environments are among the significant challenges highlighted.

Furthermore, the text offers guidance for achieving more robust outcomes in self-experimentation. It suggests using health and fitness monitoring tools for gathering precise data, acquiring books and informational resources on personal research, and employing scientific methodologies to ensure the accuracy of self-experimentation.

The text provides an array of supportive tools to aid in the systematic and accurate pursuit of self-experimentation. For instance, it neutrally mentions scientifically based books, health and fitness monitoring applications, programs for assessing sleep quality and productivity, as well as data analysis tools.

The subchapter "THE VALUE OF SELF EXPERIMENTATION" presents both the opportunities and challenges of self-experimentation as a means of personal research for personalized learning and habit improvement. It offers numerous suggestions and tools to assist in conducting self-experimentation systematically and accurately.

The text further asserts that self-experimentation can yield more precise results compared to other research studies if carried out correctly. Nonetheless, it emphasizes that self-experimentation can become problematic if the experimenter lacks the necessary technical competence. Hence, the text encourages seeking ethical approval before embarking on self-experimentation to ensure the safety of the study subject.

The text also conveys that while self-experimentation can yield valuable insights into health, the environment, and overall well-being, it is not the sole method available for obtaining these results. It suggests integrating the findings of self-experimentation with other research methods such as literature review, existing data analysis, or consultation with industry experts to attain a more comprehensive and accurate understanding of the results.

Additionally, the text underscores the importance of conducting self-experimentation in an ethical and responsible manner. This involves obtaining ethical approval, ensuring privacy, safety, and compliance with experiment conduct laws. This is particularly critical since self-experimentation may involve experimentation on oneself, which could impact the health or safety of the experimenters if not carried out correctly.

Ultimately, the text emphasizes that self-experimentation demands a high level of responsibility and preparation but can lead to significant insights into personal knowledge and habit improvement. It also recommends utilizing tools like monitoring applications or software to facilitate more accurate and methodical data collection.

SPOTTING BAD SCIENCE 101

In the subchapter titled "SPOTTING BAD SCIENCE 101," the text provides a valuable list of tips and suggestions for avoiding 'bad science' and making informed decisions regarding health and fitness. The recommended approach to tackling this subject is to maintain a healthy dose of critical skepticism when assessing scientific studies. The subchapter advises paying attention to the quality of study funding, as some studies may receive funding from private companies and, thus, be subject to conflicts of interest. Another aspect to consider is the reliability of the information source, as some sources are more trustworthy than others.

Furthermore, the text suggests carefully evaluating the number of participants in the study, its duration, and the level of randomness. These factors can influence the desired results and, therefore, the advice provided to readers. Additionally, the subchapter underscores the importance of avoiding overly sensational and extravagant claims, as they often lack a solid scientific foundation.

The text also recommends paying attention to the methods used in studies, as some of them may be flawed or inaccurate. For instance, some studies may employ too small a sample of participants, rendering them unrepresentative of the general population. Alternatively, inappropriate or non-rigorous methods could lead to false results and, consequently, reduced reliability.

To avoid falling victim to 'bad science,' the text offers the option of seeking reliable information in books or scientific publications. This allows individuals to access up-to-date and accurate information, thus avoiding the spread of misinformation.

The subchapter "SPOTTING BAD SCIENCE 101" in the text encompasses several pieces of advice and suggestions for identifying unreliable scientific studies and critically evaluating health and fitness information. Among the secondary topics addressed in the chapter are:

- The importance of refraining from deriving alarming information from unreliable sources, as such information may lack a sound analysis of data. For example, it will be highlighted that scientifically incorrect information may be disseminated on social networks or sites that employ click-baiting techniques.

- The role of conflicts of interest in research, which can lead to a substantial increase in false information. Yet, it also serves to prompt users to explore the subject matter independently.

- The significance of reproducibility in scientific research, a fundamental aspect of good research, as it allows for result verification and the ability to challenge any unreliable studies.

- The importance of science and the use of scientific sources, such as scientific publications, books, and specialized journals, where scientific work is conducted with care and attention, utilizing the correct scientific method and representing a reference point for updates and information within the relevant scientific field.

- The importance of avoiding commonplaces and generalizations that lack a scientific basis to avoid making evaluative errors.

Overall, the subchapter "SPOTTING BAD SCIENCE 101" in the text encourages the adoption of a critical approach to scientific studies, evaluating the information source, considering the quantity of participants, duration, degree of randomness, scientific validity of the methods used, and the plausibility of the claim. Paying attention to these aspects can help identify issues related to bad science and prevent making uninformed decisions regarding one's health and well-being.

SPOTTING BAD SCIENCE 102

In the subchapter "SPOTTING BAD SCIENCE 102," the text delves into the strategies employed by pharmaceutical companies to influence the opinions of both doctors and patients about their products. It's explained that these companies often sponsor clinical studies that emphasize the positive properties of their medications, presenting results in a selective and biased manner. Furthermore, it's a known practice for study results to be manipulated or even omitted to achieve the desired outcome.

Pharmaceutical companies also employ highly sophisticated marketing techniques to influence prescription decisions. These strategies include using influencer or sponsored doctors and crafting diagnostic criteria to ensure a positive diagnosis for their target drug.

The text also addresses the issue of advertising's influence on doctors, who may lack the freedom to objectively choose the best medications for their patients. Healthcare professionals are frequently swayed by advertisements and may prescribe unnecessary or ineffective medications simply because they are aggressively marketed.

Additionally, the subchapter presents various techniques to help patients and doctors identify biased clinical studies or misleading advertisements. For instance, the authors suggest sifting through study data to distinguish causal effects from side effects and considering the study's reliability. They also recommend consulting third-party sources for prescription and medication information and utilizing discussion guides with doctors to make informed decisions about the best treatment for individual patients.

One of the primary concerns described in the text is the lack of transparency from pharmaceutical companies. Access to complete study results is often difficult for doctors and patients since companies tend to publish only positive outcomes. The problem with this practice is that these studies do not represent a broader reality, potentially leading to an underestimation of a drug's real effects. The text advises paying attention to missing results or information within the studies, as these often indicate something is amiss.

Another crucial topic addressed is the use of doctors as drug representatives. Pharmaceutical companies frequently utilize doctors and other healthcare professionals as sales representatives to promote their products. This practice raises ethical concerns because it influences doctors to select what's best for the pharmaceutical company, rather than what's best for their patients. In this regard, it's vital that doctors are aware of the pressure exerted by pharmaceutical companies and can make autonomous and informed decisions regarding their patients' health.

Another critical factor that influences the assessment of drug efficacy in clinical trials is the placebo effect. Since patients expect the drug to work, this can impact their perception of the drug's effectiveness. In fact, the positive effects of drugs may stem only from this placebo effect rather than the intrinsic impact of the administered substance. Regarding this issue, the text suggests considering the placebo effect in clinical trials and paying attention to concrete scientific evidence of objective drug effects beyond the pure placebo effect.

Finally, the text touches upon the concept of seeking a new health threat, implying that there's a continuous threat to health against which only a particular drug can offer protection. The authors stress how these advertising campaigns often coincide with the over-prescription of potentially unnecessary or even harmful drugs. Often, these campaigns are geared towards boosting drug consumption rather than providing objective healthcare information.

These insights underline the complexities and potential pitfalls in the pharmaceutical industry, highlighting the importance of vigilance and a discerning approach when making decisions about healthcare.

THE SLOW-CARB DIET—194 PEOPLE

Il subchapter "THE SLOW-CARB DIET-194 PEOPLE" delves into the data regarding the Slow-Carb diet. Detailed questions were used to gather information from 194 individuals who claimed to be able to maintain this diet. The collected data encompasses various aspects, including the participants' dietary regimen, age, gender, and recorded weight loss. The subchapter analyzes this data to determine whether the Slow-Carb diet proves effective or not.

This chapter scrutinizes the data collected from these individuals, aiming to discern whether the Slow-Carb diet is genuinely capable of producing significant weight loss. Ferriss emphasizes that his research interests differ from published clinical studies on weight loss because his experiments do not employ a random sample, and they do not intend to publish this type of results.

The author seeks to identify the common characteristics shared by individuals who have succeeded with the Slow-Carb diet. One of the author's most intriguing observations is that those who adhere to this diet have a higher probability of losing weight consistently. Indeed, data analysis revealed that the subjects who lost weight followed a consistent diet, limiting their carbohydrate intake to less than 30% of total calories.

Ultimately, the subchapter compellingly demonstrates that the Slow-Carb diet seems to be an effective dietary strategy for weight loss and achieving better physical fitness. Ferriss has an array of collected data showing how the research subjects substantially and consistently achieved their weight loss goals through this dietary regimen.

In conclusion, the subchapter "THE SLOW-CARB DIET-194 PEOPLE" provides valuable data and information for anyone interested in developing a balanced and effective diet to reach their weight loss objectives.

SEX MACHINE II

In the subchapter "SEX MACHINE II," author Tim Ferriss explores two distinct protocols to enhance libido and sexual desire. The first protocol involves daily intake of fermented cod liver oil and butter rich in vitamins. The second protocol focuses on consuming high amounts of cholesterol within 20-24 hours before a planned sexual encounter. Ferriss also emphasizes the significance of cold exposure through ice baths or cold showers to influence luteinizing hormone (LH) and testosterone levels.

The primary approach involving fermented cod liver oil and butter is rooted in their high content of essential vitamins, specifically vitamins A, D, and K2. These vitamins play a crucial role in influencing sexual hormone production and reproductive health. For instance, vitamin A is necessary for proper sexual gland function and hormonal balance. Vitamin D is important for testosterone production and maintaining male fertility. Vitamin K2, while primarily associated with bone health, has also demonstrated a positive impact on sexual health.

The second approach focuses on temporarily increasing cholesterol intake within a specific timeframe before a planned sexual encounter. This method is suggested to boost libido and improve sexual health. It's important to note that high cholesterol intake is typically associated with health concerns, such as arterial plaque buildup and heart problems. Therefore, Ferriss recommends using this approach selectively, specifically for targeted, planned sexual activities.

The subchapter also explores the role of cold exposure, which can be achieved through ice baths or cold showers. Ferriss argues that cold exposure can raise LH and testosterone levels, thereby positively impacting sexual health. Notably, lower body temperature has been linked to increased testosterone levels. Additionally, cold exposure can help reduce stress and improve sleep quality, both of which are essential for sexual health.

In summary, "SEX MACHINE II" offers innovative and natural approaches to enhance sexual health through dietary choices, cold exposure, and stress reduction. It delves into secondary topics, including the significance of consuming saturated fats, regular physical exercise, and stress reduction techniques. These secondary topics provide practical insights for individuals looking to improve their sexual health and overall well-being.

THE MEATLESS MACHINE I

The subchapter titled "THE MEATLESS MACHINE I" delves into the advantages of a plant-based or meat-free diet for a span of two weeks. It explains how temporarily eliminating certain foods can be a positive restriction, leading to improved food awareness and choices. The subchapter emphasizes the removal of meat from one's diet and the lasting benefits such an experience can bring. It also touches upon the need for greater food awareness to make decisions that benefit one's health, physical performance, and the planet.

To kick things off, the subchapter zeroes in on the benefits of removing meat from your diet for roughly two weeks. It highlights how this dietary choice can become a positive constraint, ultimately enhancing your knowledge and food selections. Moreover, it underscores that a plant-based diet can be just as flavorful and nutritious, offering a wide array of food options.

Next, the subchapter discusses the importance of adopting a more mindful approach to your food choices. It warns against the pitfalls of advertising and media that often nudge people toward unhealthy, environmentally damaging food products.

It further emphasizes that being more aware of what you consume can lead to improved physical and mental performance, promoting a better physiological balance. The subchapter also delves into the environmental benefits of choosing a plant-based diet, asserting that such a choice can reduce the overall environmental footprint in numerous ways, including the reduction of greenhouse gases and food waste.

Another key point the text addresses is the significance of experimenting with your diet to find what best suits your lifestyle.

It encourages making food choices independently and responsibly, free from societal pressures or advertisements.

Furthermore, the text argues that opting for a plant-based or meat-free diet is not a limiting choice, but rather an opportunity to diversify your food palate. It underscores how a wide range of plant-based foods can be just as tasty and nourishing as animal-based products, offering the chance to explore new flavors and options.

Additionally, it advocates trying a plant-based or meatless diet for a brief period, say two weeks, to assess whether this dietary approach aligns with your lifestyle. It highlights that this approach need not be permanent but can serve as an opportunity to evaluate the positive effects on health, psychological well-being, and the surrounding environment.

Another pertinent point in the subchapter pertains to the health benefits associated with reduced meat and animal product consumption. It cites numerous studies that have shown a high intake of red meat can increase the risk of cardiovascular diseases, type 2 diabetes, and cancer. Conversely, a plant-based diet can mitigate these risks while boosting physical and mental energy.

The subchapter underscores the necessity of heightened food awareness and the impact of dietary choices on the environment. It highlights how a plant-based diet can reduce the global environmental footprint in several ways, including the reduction of greenhouse gases, food waste, preservation of water resources, and animal welfare.

In conclusion, "THE MEATLESS MACHINE I" provides valuable insights into the myriad benefits of adopting a plant-based or meat-free diet. This choice not only promotes individual health but also contributes to reducing the impact on the surrounding environment.

THE MEATLESS MACHINE II

"The Meatless Machine II" subchapter unveils a 28-day experiment by John Berardi, a nutritional biochemistry expert, who decided to go 100% vegan, despite being a meat-eater. The objective was to increase muscle mass without consuming meat, a primary protein source.

Berardi shares his experience during the experiment and delves into the dietary strategies he adopted. He zeroed in on plant-based proteins, such as legumes, chia seeds, and hemp seeds. Simultaneously, he limited carbohydrate intake to reduce inflammation and trigger the production of anabolic hormones.

To compensate for the calorie deficit due to calorie restriction, Berardi increased his intake of healthy fats, like avocado and coconut oils. The aim was to enter a ketogenic state, wherein the body uses fats as an energy source instead of carbohydrates.

The subchapter also outlines the foods Berardi consumed during the 28-day vegan diet. His diet featured numerous plant-based foods, including quinoa, sweet potatoes, and avocados. He opted for home-cooked meals instead of relying on restaurant vegan options.
Berardi reports the results of his experiment. Over the 28-day period, he documented a significant increase in muscle mass and a reduction in body fat compared to his pre-vegan diet. He also reported a marked improvement in overall health, with less inflammation and joint pain.

An essential secondary point in this subchapter revolves around the significance of plant-based proteins in a vegan diet. Berardi's emphasis on legumes, seeds, quinoa, and other plant-based foods demonstrates that a well-balanced vegan diet can provide all the necessary proteins for muscle building.

Another crucial theme is the relationship between fats and health. Berardi challenged the conventional notion of fats as "bad" for health, highlighting that fats can be a vital source of energy and nourishment. He focused on healthy fats, like avocado and coconut oils, to maintain a consistent calorie intake throughout the experiment.

A further secondary topic pertains to the importance of daily calorie planning. With meat eliminated from his diet, Berardi needed to find alternative protein sources to compensate for the protein deficit. His dietary regime necessitated meticulous planning of fat intake. He utilized a calorie-counting app to track daily calorie consumption.

Berardi underscored the importance of food variety in a vegan diet. Rather than restricting himself to a few staple foods, he chose to incorporate a wide range of foods to ensure he received all the necessary vitamins and minerals.

In conclusion, "The Meatless Machine II" subchapter within the selected text provides a wealth of information on vegan diets and dietary strategies crucial for muscle building and overall health. Secondary topics such as the significance of plant-based proteins, healthy fats, daily calorie planning, food variety, and the commitment required are all essential in achieving the best results.

Conclusion

Your Ongoing Journey to a Transformed Life.
In the pages of "Summary of The 4-Hour Body" by Tim Ferriss, you have embarked on a captivating exploration of what it truly means to unlock the potential of your body and redefine the limits of your health, fitness, and longevity. As we reach the conclusion of this book, it's essential to recognize that this is not the end but rather a stepping stone on your path to continuous self-improvement and self-discovery.

Ferriss has shared with us a treasure trove of unconventional yet scientifically sound strategies to optimize our lives. Through his relentless pursuit of knowledge and experimentation, he has illuminated a fascinating world where the seemingly impossible becomes achievable.

The principles and techniques presented here are not just information to be consumed but tools to be wielded in your journey towards a healthier, more vibrant, and ultimately fulfilling life. The essence of "The 4-Hour Body" is not merely a set of ideas; it's a way of life, an attitude of unwavering curiosity and a relentless commitment to being the best version of yourself.

As you leave these pages behind and venture into the world, remember that the pursuit of health and self-improvement is an ongoing process. It's a journey with no final destination but an infinite path towards self-discovery and transformation. You hold the power to shape your body, your health, and your destiny.

Your copy of "Summary of The 4-Hour Body" is your key to this extraordinary adventure. With the knowledge you've gained and the tools you've discovered, you have the potential to sculpt the life you desire. Embrace the challenges that lie ahead, welcome the opportunity for transformation, and **dare** to push the boundaries of what you believe is achievable.

This book is not just a source of wisdom; it's a mindset and a way of life. It embodies the belief that each of us has the capability to achieve remarkable feats and redefine the possibilities of health and fitness. We hold the power to shape our destinies and redefine our lives.

So, as you step away from these pages, remember that your journey to a 4-hour body and a life well-lived continues. The quest for greatness is ongoing, and the pursuit of health and well-being knows no bounds. Embrace each challenge, celebrate every triumph, and let your journey be a testament to what's possible.

Thank you for embarking on this extraordinary adventure with us. May your pursuit of greatness be relentless, your path towards health and well-being be filled with triumphs beyond imagination, and your life be an ever-evolving masterpiece of vitality and fulfillment.

Safe travels on your remarkable journey to a transformed life.

Thank you for purchasing this book.

If you enjoyed it, please leave a brief review. Your feedback is important to us and will help other readers decide whether to read the book too.

For a small company like us, getting reviews (especially on Amazon) means a lot to us. We can't THANK YOU enough for this!

About PrimeInsight Press

At PrimeInsight Press, our story begins as a passionate small team with a belief: knowledge, when shared with passion, can change the world. We have dedicated ourselves to creating enlightening workbooks, authentic, and professional guides, also paying special attention to their high-quality, engaging interior design.

We believe that every workbook is an opportunity to touch hearts and empower minds. Through the pages of our workbooks, we hope to inspire you to dream and provide you with the tools to bring those dreams to life.

Join us at PrimeInsight Press, and together, transform your journey of growth, one page at a time.

SCAN the QR Code
to Enjoy the Audiobook